Hello L,

I appreciate your pu..... my book.

Although validation should not be important at my age, it is.

I hope you find some useful thoughts in these pages.

Think Good Thoughts
Richard

"Richard's wealth of experience can enrich every area of your life. This enjoyable book is a user-friendly road map to success, with tools you can implement at any stage and any age to create the results you want."

–**Tanya Chernova**,
Co-Author, #1 Best-Seller, *UnderMind*,
Global Speaker and Canada's Top 100 Most Powerful Women
CEO, Tanya Chernova Global Corp.

"Like little gifts to unwrap each day, Richard has inspired me to live with intentionality. Pick up this book, and you'll find yourself picked up!"

–**David Lewis**,
Best-Selling Author, *The Emerging Leader: Eight Lessons for Life in Leadership*,
Vice President of Franchising, Express Employment Professionals

"Well done, Richard! We all need those friendly reminders and moments to breathe! You've captured that in your book and journey. Congratulations!"

–**Kari Lywood**,
President/Sr. Client Lead, Kari Lywood Events and KL Group

"If you know Richard, then you know his contagious enthusiasm, which comes through loud and clear in this book. A great daily read with short lessons to ponder throughout the day. Grab a journal and let your pen answer all the questions he has coming at you."

–**Maria Weber**,
Brands Manager, TFB & Associates Ltd.
Food Importer and Distributor

"With a sense of humour, a realistic approach to becoming the best you can be and some musical references that spin some wisdom, Richard Morin invites us to take control of our lives in the here and now and for many years to come. His ideas, when implemented, will help you to live a richer life."

–**Wayne Vanwyck**,
Founder, The Achievement Centre

"Well, I must say that after reading Rich Morin's book, *You Working With You, I* had an extra jump in my step. Rich's life perspective delivered with his direct candor refocused my thinking and caused me to change some negative patterns that had crept in. Great job, Rich. An effective book with focused life lessons for those just starting out and for those who need <u>that</u> reminder on how to accomplish great things."

–**Wayne Clancy**,
Founder and Chief Innovation Officer,
MindSuiteMetrics.com and Future Strategies Inc.

YOU
WORKING WITH
YOU

YOU WORKING WITH YOU

A Roadmap to Self Mastery

RICHARD MORIN

NEXT CENTURY
PUBLISHING

You Working With You
A Roadmap to Self Mastery

Copyright ©2016 by Richard Morin
All rights reserved.

Published by Next Century Publishing
Las Vegas, Nevada
www.NextCenturyPublishing.com

No part of this publication may be reproduced, stored in a retrieval system, or transmitted in any form or by any means—electronic, mechanical, photocopy, recording, or any other—without the prior permission of the author.

ISBN: 978-1-68102-151-5
Library of Congress Control Number: 2016941101

Printed in the United States of America

TABLE OF CONTENTS

Acknowledgments 13
Introduction 15

I: INTRODUCING...YOU! 19

What is it like to be you?... 21
Words: Do they work for you, or against you?............................ 23
Your mission statement: words that define your trajectory........... 27
Telepathy: You and I, connected 29
Waking up 31
New Year's Eve is every day 33
Life is improvisation in real time,
   requiring that you be in the moment. 35
Operation and care manual on YOU 38
Life is an inside job 40
The mirror.. 42
Destiny (What is yours?).. 45
Your plot line: The one you develop as you work
   through your life.. 47
The journey; finding or creating oneself? (Or both?).................. 50
Being the driver in your life 52
For every mile of road, there are two miles of ditch 54
Happiness 58
Mediocrity versus greatness 62
Between stimulus and response, there is a gap.
   Live in the gap. 64

II: THE SPOTLIGHT IS ON YOU 69

Roles played each day and throughout your life 70

YOU Inc.: self-development using a SWOT analysis 73

You working with YOU
and others (The work required to play) 76

Harmony, as a result of being able to work with
yourself and others 80

All business is people business 83

First impression / last impression 86

Managers, coaches, leaders and parents 88

Mentor 91

Listen, seek to understand 93

Dealing with issues 95

Popularity 99

Instant Gratification 101

Do your job.
(This might have been the title of the book, but …) 103

Productivity/work ethic 106

Quality 109

Experience? 111

Confidence 113

Earning money versus making money:
People vote with their dollars. 115

Selling? Not What You Do? 117

Momentum, prolonged success 120

Competition 122

Distractions 124

Compromise 127

III: WHAT'S HOLDING YOU BACK? 131

Checking in 132

Life is hard 134

Bullying 136

Forgive and forget 139

Life is not fair 141

Consequences 143

Wish you were better rather than things being easier 147

"A bird searching for a cage" (blog by Seth Godin) 149

Obstacles to YOU being in the moment, as in here and now 151

Meditation 154

Thinking good thoughts (What other kinds are there?) 158

Hanging on (perspective) 161

"When you are going through hell, keep going."
   Winston Churchill 163

Silence and reflection 165

Mental and physical journey:
   What you think and do is up to you. 167

You Settling for less? Why? 169

Your firewall: No one can make you feel
   inferior without your consent. 171

Suffering 173

Internal conflict (anxiety) 175

One day at a time 179

Reflection: A considered life 181

Privilege 183

IV: MAKING CHANGES 185

CHANGE: It's all around you and happens every day. 186
Have you type-casted yourself? Why? 190
Perception and reality 193
Course correction 195
Making decisions and commitments 197
Urgent versus important 200
Circle of influence versus the circle of concern 202
"Stupid is as stupid does"? Not quite. 205
Spending versus investing time 207
Your personal scale 209
Stick to that commitment 211
Discipline, or more importantly, self-discipline
  (Don't ever get tired of this word — ever!) 214
Practice (10,000 hours: Malcolm Gladwell) 216
Nutrition and consumption 218
Distractions 221
Blinders 223
Habits, according to Charles Duhigg 225
Information gathering or solution mode? 227
Courage 229
Believing, after all, requires so much less effort than thinking. .. 231
What's holding you back? You? 234
Why not you, why not now?
  (Be, have, learn, enjoy, see, hear, taste, work…now) 236
The END 238

EPILOGUE 241

Death: A taboo subject for some? 242
About the Author 245

YOU
WORKING WITH
YOU

ACKNOWLEDGMENTS

I would like to thank those who helped me see my way through the maze of writing a book.

My lovely wife, Sylviane, who never doubted me, and in fact pushed me along.

My dear mother, Marie Ange Morin, whose picture sits on my desk, with a continual smile at my efforts.

My dad, who is never surprised at the various adventures I have thrown myself into.

Andree Cote, who used her years of teaching and reading to provide sage advice.

Paul Tyndall, who pointed out the stark realities of writing and selling a book, motivating me even more to get my thoughts into print.

Simon Presland, my Editor in Chief, whose patience and support on my many phone calls kept me buoyed.

INTRODUCTION

You are given two things in life for free, your life, and time. You receive both upon arrival, and lose both at the same time. What you do with them is up to you.

This book is all about you — your life, your time, your story, your challenges, your successes and all those things that make you, you. What could be more interesting than that? How do you like you, so far?

Think about it, why not you? You only go around once in life, so why not have those things you want? Why not be the person you want to be by reflecting, correcting your trajectory and applying energy as you work to make your future, your reality, by your choice? Imagine you are at the controls of your own life, well … you are! Now what will you do?

Is change a challenge for you as you move from year to year, and strive to be more? Do you do the same things the same way, and do you ever wonder how far can you go?

What is your destiny? What are you destined to do, or not do? Have you captured the essence of what you want your destiny to be? Do you even realize you have the power to create your own destiny?

Each section and vignette you are about to read is written to inspire you to think big, to dream big, and to live big, as defined by you. Enjoy the words you're about to read, and ponder on them throughout your day. If you happen to make a few adjustments that result in a more favourable outcome in your life, then good for you. If you simply find the book entertaining that is great as well. I'm not looking to drag anybody into anything, but to simply pass on some of the things that I have learned or have thought about on my journey through life.

We need more leaders in the world, but before you can lead others you have to be able to lead yourself. And leadership starts with our thought-life. So think good thoughts — it's a choice you can make starting today!

If you have purchased this book for yourself, or bought it for your significant other, a friend, family member, employee or even your boss, it might be because harmony is missing. Perhaps you feel disconnected, or see disconnection in others. Life is out of sync. Perhaps it is way too repetitive. Or maybe there is simply a lack of awareness.

Most books are like a travel atlas or a map app on your electronic device. They show the roads you might take, but the terrain and details are left out, and it is in the details that contain your answers. These details require thoughtful analysis from time to time, an "un-plugging" from everything that conspires to keep you "full" when silent moments of reflection and meditation would provide soothing silence, leading to an understanding of self.

In your heart you know you are good, and you're worthy of the things you want, but as you interact with others you somehow lose touch with yourself, and end up choosing words and saying things that are out of character. You do things that make others scratch their heads at what you have just said or done.

People have dropped hints, and you have pondered their words trying to merge their values into your life. As each day unfolds, you find yourself evaluating too much instead of just going with the flow.

It is unfair to compare yourself with anyone else. We are all different. If you were to ask some of the people you look up to why they are so comfortable in their own skin, you may find this is not the case. If they were honest, you would find that almost everyone is searching, working with and within themselves. They may even strain to find the words that best capture the essence of what your question has unearthed, because they are never as comfortable as they seem.

Is the face you see in the mirror a true reflection of all that is you?

Think of Lord Farquaad in SHREK who had the talking mirror produce what suited him at the risk of getting smashed by one of the Lord's henchmen. You don't want to be like him.

You are working with yourself. But are you playing a role in a sitcom, play, drama, action, adventure, or mystery? Or is there a mix? This is life — your life we are talking about. In real time there are no re-takes. How do you get better at being you? It is imperative that you keep on living, growing, challenging and working with yourself, practicing in real time. Every day is a new take, and with each day comes the opportunity to do things differently based on what is coming at you. Remember, you get to choose.

As you dress for the day and fix your mind on the roles you are about to play, you look for cues as to how you are doing. Are you being accepted? Are people smiling and enjoying your words, expressions and actions? The truth is, if you are focused on getting the approval of others, you will never focus on the task at hand — growing and changing and becoming the person you want to be. Instead, you will continuously search for acceptance and approval in the eyes and expressions of those who see you, trying to continually adjust.

Remember that the slimiest, lying, cheating, smiling, and most persistent politician who kisses every grandmother and hugs every child might get 60 percent of the popular vote. So don't be hard on yourself if you fall short of your expectations. 100 percent acceptance is impossible. However, you can always be friendly and accept the outcome.

At the conclusion of each day take a moment to reflect on the events and people you were a part of. If you write down one lesson learned each day, you will create a list of lessons that will help you in the future.

Practice does not improve your abilities and game; perfect practice is what takes you to the next level. I know people who have practiced on the golf course every day, and years later their score never changed. Why? Because they are strengthening the same things they have always done, thereby reinforcing the very things that they want to improve on. History for them repeats itself every day.

In the book titled *The Art of War* by Sun Tzu (translated by Thomas Cleary) you learn that conflict, aggression, wars never need to happen, and that conflict is un-necessary. It goes on to illustrate that success and victory favour the prepared; that although you plan for positive outcomes in your life, you are also prepared for unforeseen circumstances.

Conflict, fighting, argument, war should always be a last resort, because nothing good comes out of them.

Whatever endeavor they are in, successful people, families, and companies are successful because they work with people in a spirit of harmony, cultivating a shared vision and enlisting others to join in and participate in mutually beneficial activities. Is there competition for all things in your life? Yes of course, but such is life. Be prepared.

Enjoy today; it is yours to do with as you wish. Treat each day as if it were your last — because one never knows. Think of the song titled "It's a good life" by Aaron Garner, and reflect on his words.

As you begin to read this book, I'd like to challenge you with a couple of questions:

Q: Are you adept at letting go of the past having learned from your passage through it?

Q: Can you build momentum through getting things done, each new day?

I: INTRODUCING...YOU!

WHAT IS IT LIKE TO BE YOU?

Nobody knows exactly what it's like to be you. Everything you have experienced, heard or seen has an impact on the way only you think and see things. Your parents, siblings, relatives, friends, your family's financial standing, school, in which part of the world you grew up, under which political party's leadership and whether your country was at war, along with a bunch of other important ingredients, all went into making the current version of you.

So how can anyone else tell you what activities in which you can excel, or where you should fit in? How can anybody else know how you personally feel in certain circumstances or situations and then proceed to tell you how you should act accordingly? Do they mean like them? To whom can they be referring?

Your life is personal — there is no one else like you in the entire world. Having said this, why do you keep on comparing yourself to others? How can you mistakenly believe you should be like, act like, look like, or even think like someone else?

It is impossible.

Live your life without the good opinion of others.

In his book *How to Stop Acting*, Harold Guskin gives examples of great actors who finally learned to say the lines of their scripts and dress the part while doing it in the way they feel the character should or would do those things. It is the originality of the actor that earns them more and more roles and helps them avoid being typecast in one particular role or genre. The great actors understand the storyline and its ever-changing rhythms and adjust to suit the fluidity of it all.

You are the same, or should be in your life. You have the option of staying with the tried and proven ways you have been acting, or you can venture out a little and test the limits of your creativity in speech, vocabulary, and ways of responding to stimuli. You basically allow the moment determine your next move instead of being one-dimensional and predictable.

Who you are now, is not the same as who you were five, ten, fifteen, even twenty years ago. You will be different again in five, ten, fifteen, or twenty from now. If you want there to be a difference, there will be.

To move forward, though, you have to move. Does this make sense? If forward movement is equal to progression, and to progress means to be in a different place from where you are now, then move on instead of wasting your energy trying to keep the past with you. Leave the past behind you — just like what you see in the rear-view mirror as you drive. The past is not something you can take with you. So, why try?

Think of the Moody Blues song, "The Actor."

Flexibility, an open mind, and a new day, every day. What will you do or say today, in what way?

WORDS: DO THEY WORK FOR YOU, OR AGAINST YOU?

Words are the foundation of what makes you competent as a human, and renders you able to communicate and apply some self-determination in your life.

Think of those song lyrics you love to listen to and sing. Why did the writer select those words, in that particular order? What about the chorus? What is the chorus or theme to your life, what words have you enlisted to define you and your life?

Often people are careless with their words, and, sadly, some people seem to miss the connection with the words they put out there, and with which they are labelled.

Words mirror the person choosing, and then using, them. What are the key words you would use to define you?

These words can include the following: honest, hardworking, fair, open, friendly, fun, intelligent, resourceful, healthy, strong, fit, disciplined, a good listener, powerful speaker, timid, mousey, careful, crazy; a joker, trickster, team player, clown, musician, lover, good worker, good father/mother, respectful, selfless … the list can go on and on.

How do the words on your list get there? Are they permanently etched in stone or are they transient whereby they appear sometimes but not others? What are the words that others would use to define you? How many from your list would be on their list? Would you be surprised to hear some of the words others would use to paint their image of you?

How different are the words you would now use versus the words you made use of five, ten, or twenty years ago or when you were a child? Is there a difference? Knowing the words and then speaking or writing them is one thing. Living them is totally different, as it requires the pure intent to make the words part of your daily reality.

If you choose "honest" as a key word, then be honest, in all of your dealings. By being honest with others, the returning result will be in form of trust. People will see you as honest and label you as such up until the day you die. Furthermore, the label will be mentioned at your wake and perhaps be etched on your tombstone.

What if you wrote your eulogy today, posted it by your door or on your computer screen-saver where you can see it at various times throughout the day? Would you, or could you, live those words today and every other day of your life, making them real and relevant to you?

Be careful as to which words you give to yourself. It is better to define yourself than be defined by others in less than desirable ways.

A short story for you: It was a dark, cold morning — about 5 a.m. — as I was driving alone on a desolate two lane highway in the dead of winter with snow banks six feet high, listening to a radio talk show where they were discussing books, life and how those are captured in words. The main speaker was a smoker. I could hear him draw in and then exhale between thoughts. At one point there was a longer pause and then he said, "Every word, is a stain on silence." Wow!

I have struggled to contain my outflow ever since then, but at times I remain a stain master. (Do you have this tendency?)

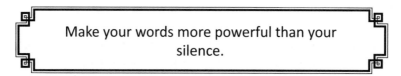

Before you open your mouth, there is silence. As long as you or others remain that way, the silence continues. Beautiful silence allows you to think or create. Imagine that.

Now what is it you so desperately want to say? Why do you want to say it that way? How else can you frame your thoughts so that you are clear and explanatory, and leave no room for misunderstanding? Be careful here: this is your chance to emblazon history with words that will last forever — provided that someone can perfectly remember those exact words. If, however, what you said gets written down in some form … then all bets are off.

So, go ahead, think, speak, or write. Ha ha! Good luck with that … we are all veritable stain masters, capable of leaving no silence unblemished.

Your words and actions of course, make up your legacy. Don't you think you ought to be more mindful with those moments you stain?

What do you want people to say at your wake? The answer is simple: they will use whatever fodder you have provided them during your tenure here on Earth.

Politicians seem to be immune to this stain on silence thing, because the moment they are quoted as making some promise that winds up unfulfilled or broken, they say something to the effect of, "Gee, I did not say that." or "That is not what I meant." or some other rubbish in an attempt to brush aside responsibility for their own words.

If you love someone, say it clearly with the right intonation and body language. Otherwise, your words will fall short of the target — sort of like bullets at a firing range falling into the sand long before the target is reached.

If the word "try" is part of your vocabulary, get rid of it. As the Star Wars character Yoda once said, "Do or do not. There is no try." The word *try* is worthless — useless, without value and a waste of your breath and the attention. A three-letter lie.

Words. Choose them, say them with the full accompaniment of emotions and heartfelt truth. Or let them linger in the dark part of your mind where eventually they will fade away.

Think of the Hal Urban book, Positive Words, Powerful Results.

Or think of the Ringo Starr song, "It Don't Come Easy."
("Gotta pay your dues if you ... ")

> Words, we live by them and die with them.
> Be careful.

YOUR MISSION STATEMENT: WORDS THAT DEFINE YOUR TRAJECTORY

You might think that mission statements solely belong within a corporate environment, only festooning the vestibules or hallways of Fortune 500 companies or perhaps in the office of the president, but certainly not relevant to you. You might be right about the first part of that statement, but you are wrong about the second part.

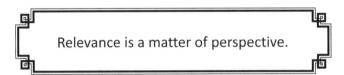

Relevance is a matter of perspective.

For those companies to exist and prosper, and for the firms' presidents to proudly display framed replicas in their offices, the mission statements you see have long been a part of the people who work there, helping to lead them to where they are now.

Mission statements and clearly defined goals share a common link. Like a map made available for the person or company to use, mission statements and clearly defined goals can play a huge role in the lives of the people who write these words, and then choose to make them real through their daily actions.

Sometimes people and companies lose their way. Distractions and loss of focus can send businesses adrift toward mediocrity and failure — causing undue harm to any associated stakeholders.

A mission statement is akin to a recipe for a tasty dish. It takes time to prepare; you have to select cookware; follow the listed ingredients using the correct amounts, choose oven or microwave temperatures and exact cooking times; know how much stirring is needed; and add whichever spices are required in the proper sequence so that they are not ruined by too much heat and, thus, leave your dish lacking taste.

Your life is not much different. Ask yourself: *Am I cooking? Am I involved in the process and providing ingredients, or just showing up in time to consume whatever life serves up?*

When you understand the value of goals and mission statements and apply them to your life, you will achieve greater success. Think of goals and mission statements like a compass with which you can refer when needed.

So ... what is your mission statement? What are the guiding principles that define you, your company and perhaps your family?

Life is a creative process. Experiment just as a cook does with ingredients, and you will take your life in new directions. Revisit your mission statement as time goes on and ensure it is relevant with your current situation and capabilities.

Think of the Sting song, "Something The Boy Said."

TELEPATHY: YOU AND I, CONNECTED

There you are, sitting in your living room, or standing on your porch or balcony leaning on the rail, commuting, riding a stationary bike (a real bike and reading just leads to pain and suffering) or doing whatever. In your hands is this book. With you reading what I have written, we are connected. Can you feel the connection?

Think of how conversations work. Other people share a story, some facts, or opinions, and you feel a connection, or not. By your reading of this book, there is a telepathic conversation taking place. (The one difference is this: if you want to offer a rebuttal, I suggest making some notes and coming to a book-signing event; perhaps we can take a moment to speak.)

I have written this some time ago, and the gap between me writing and you reading will vary greatly depending on our circumstances. And yet, it does not matter; telepathy is at play as you will see the same words as written by me, and follow along with my line of thought in (mostly) the way I intended. We are connected.

You will see the things that I see and feel many of the same emotions as we explore the use of words I have laid down in the fashion that I have applied them. You and I will be connected in a way that even some of your friends might like to be, but haven't based on your unwillingness to share your most intimate thoughts and feelings. What is it that you are afraid of? Be honest with yourself, and wear your honesty with pride.

Our goal is to explore, and dig into life — with all of its possibilities — in as many ways as we can. In the process, we hope to establish a new truth for you based on your current age, situation, abilities and strengths, and all of the other ever-changing elements that make you what you are.

I have purposely not spelled out everything in a detailed fashion. My aspiration is that you will fill in the blanks, create your own answers to the questions I have offered and come away with a more rounded view of you.

I can see someone who is intent on discovering more about life and how they fit into it. You are reading this and making notes in the margins, forging plans, and stepping out of your shadow in part because you are more aware that

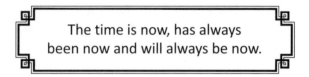

The time is now, has always been now and will always be now.

There you are in your life, with so many other potential outcomes available to you. Slowly you are turning away the doubts, your friends' warnings that "you should be careful," your concerns that something might happen (I sure hope something will happen), and your fear of the unknown. Instead, you are taking tentative steps toward living in the present moment with all of its potential.

An old saying that captures this thought goes: Life is like driving at night, you only get to see 500 feet in front of you hence two hands on the wheel, and the rear view mirror is of no value.

Think of the Pink Floyd song, "Your Possible Pasts."

Can you feel me?

WAKING UP

When you wake up, what are the first words you utter, or think? Are they words of optimism and power based on your zest for life and your focus on goals to accomplish? Or are they words of the negative sort, with connotations of anger and frustration, pain and despair?

Which was it? Really?

Waking up to the possibilities in your life requires some effort to see what lies in front of you. It is you who has to wake up from all that has happened before this moment, and realize that it is now a new day. What happened yesterday and the days before that are in the past and remain there unless you choose to carry over those old thoughts and actions.

Through which lens are you looking as you awake each day? Yesterday's? Last week's? Or … do you spend this new day peeking through your binoculars to scope out the terrain ahead to ensure you pick the correct path you wish to take?

Much like your morning shower and cleansing routine, waking up to the now is not very different. It requires the scrubbing off yesterday's sweat and grime, cleansing the skin and starting fresh.

Songs, lyrics, books, movies, plays and life itself offer up opportunities aplenty to latch onto an idea, not relinquishing your hold until you choose to let go.

Do you need waking up? What reality would you like to wake up to every day? Ahh yes, take a moment, start out with a word, then another, then another and build up your vision on paper and enjoy the process of waking up and making good use of your waking hours.

Richard Morin

Hello, good morning, go ahead, do it.

Think of the Pink Floyd song, "Time."

NEW YEAR'S EVE IS EVERY DAY

If there is one day that contains so much in the way of hope, angst, promise, freedom from those things you are dealing with, a chance to start over again and get it right, an opportunity to make good on promises made to yourself and others, it is New Year's Eve. (You could also lump a wedding day into this category.)

The problem with New Year's Eve is that you wrongly think that, with the bell tolling at midnight, the new dawn will automatically bring you that new lease on life, ways to have better control over your emotions, willpower to support your vast plans, hopes and dreams, and freedom from all those long-time bad dependencies and habits that have been harming your mind and body.

All this to take place in one day? Really? WOW!

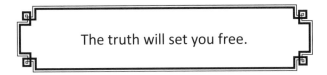

The truth will set you free.

The truth is that every day is New Year's Day. To borrow an axiom from the people at Alcoholics Anonymous who have lived this reality every day of their lives, it is always one day at a time, and you can start anytime you want. You do NOT have to wait till next New Year's Eve to address your issues, or tackle your opportunities.

Now that you are free from the waiting period until the next New Year's Eve comes around, and the pressure that one day sets on your shoulders, pick one of the issues or quests you want to work with and get started. Now.

Ten, a hundred, a thousand, or even ten thousand days on, you will be able to celebrate the fact that you used your thinking capabilities to develop your willpower and take control of your life. To be honest, that willpower was always there; perhaps you had let it shrink until it was practically invisible.

The best way to learn in a deep fashion is to teach. Not that you want to become a raving, raging Messiah screaming out your message on a street corner, or constantly chirping on about how you have found yourself and are now anointed with the power to help others.

You will, with time, lead people by your actions and your strengths. When they come to you, asking for your thoughts on how to deal with various issues, you will then be able to teach to what is now a willing audience.

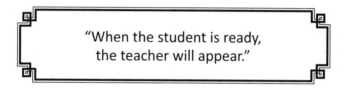

"When the student is ready, the teacher will appear."

This old saying can also apply to your life and the lives of others time and again. If you had acted on all of the lessons all of the well-meaning people in your life had offered you, you might have been able to avoid some of the pain and hardship you went through, but … who has the time to listen to advice for which you have not asked?

When next New Year's Eve arrives, have fun, enjoy the evening, be with friends and loved ones. Instead of burdening yourself with hollow promises, uttered in either a Champagne-induced haze or panic-induced throes of stress and anxiety, smile at the fact that New Year's Eve is just another day in a string of them and that you don't need this particular day to motivate you into action.

Are you ready, now? Had enough? OK, go for it!

Think of the Eagles song, "No More Cloudy Days."

LIFE IS IMPROVISATION IN REAL TIME, REQUIRING THAT YOU BE IN THE MOMENT.

Life is improvisation or "improv" in real time, all of the time. You simply do not know what is about to come your way. When something does happen, you will have a fleeting moment, in the gap, to engage it, look at it, ignore it or work with it.

How you react to that something depends on your interpretation and can be categorized by any of these words: threatening, insulting, enlightening, humorous, fun …. These can also include gestures, facial expressions, actions complete with props, or anything else that you or the people who enter the various stages of your life have at their disposal.

Each person has something to offer and it is up to you whether or not to use it and move on in sync with them, or not. These people are often unaware of how they are viewed, and because none of this is rehearsed, you have to be adept at falling in stride with them or not.

The basic rule of "improv," as you see on TV or in comedy acts, is to always say "yes!"

"Yes" opens doors, allows for a continuation of the conversation thought or action, and brings people together.

"No," on the other hand, means no. No continuation, no communication, and nowhere to go.

Think of "yes" like a green light at an intersection where you get to continue on your journey. Think of "no" as a red light that stops all movement and holds you in place.

If you watch movies, TV sitcoms, dramas, etc., you see that the good ones have flow between the actors, and that "yes" keeps things moving, whereas "no" stops the action, or causes a sharp change in chemistry.

Take a social situation, for example. There are maybe two or three people that you know well, but a lot more that you don't know. What is your typical style or modus operandi? Are you apt to walk up to someone new, a stranger, stick out your hand, and say something like, "Hi! I am so and so and I thought I would introduce myself. What is your name?"

Really? Why not? What do you have to lose, and what is there to gain? I would suggest that you have everything to gain and absolutely nothing to lose. This is a tremendous opportunity to learn about someone else, improve your social skills and broadening your range of friends and acquaintances.

Once you meet new people, and learn to play along with their words and expressions, you will be miles ahead of where you were before. Would you rather be stuck in a small pond with a few fish, or swimming in a vast ocean where there are unlimited fish?

The caveat here is that you must improve your abilities and confidence in order to roll from role to role throughout your day, and be very flexible and confident even while playing father, mother, friend, employee, son, daughter, manager, player … and this happens every day of your life.

There are things you must do in your day and life that involves people. How you do them and in what spirit are up to you. The choice starts with a "yes" and continue on, or a "no" followed by an immediate stoppage.

Just like music in which the band of your choice plays in sync, each member and instrument in tune with the others, and all contributing to the end result of the song in play. These musicians did not just pick up a guitar and walk up to the microphone. They practised, faced hostile crowds early on when their playing was not what it is now, but kept up their mastery, and learned, practised, practised some more, and now they are where they are, playing for you, going from "yes" to "yes" as they blend in with each other.

Living life from the perspective of being in an acting group, playing a skit in the mode of improv, is reality. It is happening in real time. Get on with it. This never gets old, as there are always new players entering your life, even if they come uninvited.

Practice with your friends and family, at work, with strangers ... stay with "yes" and work with the possibilities that come as a result and you will learn how to roll with the punches, weave when you have to and take a blow sometimes while having a great time.

Think of the Supertramp song, "Rudy."

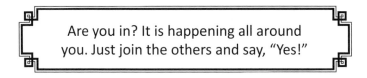

Are you in? It is happening all around you. Just join the others and say, "Yes!"

Can you think of a situation where for whatever reason you sent out a "no," when upon reflection a "yes" would have been the better, more appropriate response?

OPERATION AND CARE MANUAL ON YOU

When you arrived on this planet, everything was fully functional. Well … perhaps size, knowledge, abilities, skills, personality, fears, doubts, concerns, and one's bathroom capabilities were not instilled in you yet, but would soon be in place.

Your well-meaning parents, guardians, siblings, babysitters, employers, church, government, school … all did what they did, good or bad to render you to the point where you are now. But there is so much more ahead of you. Can you see it?

There was no owner's manual explaining how to operate or motivate you, or control and prepare you for what lay ahead after your birth. Here you are now at whatever age you are — fifteen, twenty, thirty, forty, fifty, sixty, seventy — and still no operational manual. But how could there be?

Nobody to tell or guide you, or aid you as you progress along linear time lines that never vary and never stop. The time is always "nownownownownownow**NOW**nownownow!"

What time is it, now?

If there was such a manual, it could contain a couple of chapters on maintenance, nutrition, learning, love, work, family, and a myriad of other titles. But the largest single chapter which would be called "Your Future" would be blank. Who could have written an accurate depiction about how you could be utilized, for what purpose, and to what end?

If you were to write such a manual on how to properly apply you (your body and mind), what would it include? Who reads a manual anyway when buying anything new? Do you?

Think of the song, "Nothing I Can Do About It Now"
by Willie Nelson.

Be good to yourself, pull the right strings and enjoy the results you generate.

LIFE IS AN INSIDE JOB

Who you are as you is much more important than how you appear to be.

Are you kind? Caring? Social? Friendly? Hard working? Helpful? Willing to learn? Willing to share? Willing to contribute?

Are you a team player? Can you and do you contribute to your family, team, school, job, city, town or village?

Do you apply your voice towards the betterment of the world at large while not being afraid to tackle the less salient topics (such as women's rights worldwide)?

While one's appearance — and all the time and attention devoted to looking our best — plays a role in our lives, people will ultimately remember you for the things you did and said and how you made others feel.

Being pretty or handsome, possessing a great body and wearing sharp clothing is a bonus. But what good does any of that do you if you're considered nasty, lazy, a liar, cheater, and someone who spends too much mirror time trying to look even more impressive on the outside?

Take a good, hard look at yourself. If you are pleased with both the outside and inside of you, then enjoy and put your best effort into your life. If what you see on either your exterior or interior needs work, then get on it.

What are you reading? With what are you filling your mind? To whom are you listening? Are you thinking good thoughts?

It is much easier to build muscle or go to a tanning parlor. However, even those things fade without more time in the gym or on the tanning bed. The real you — the thinking, smiling, sharing, friendly and good-natured you — requires similar efforts, but the end results are long-lasting and so worth the investment of time. The results can be measured in friends, loved ones, by your employer, and so many other ways.

Learn to take the time to listen and understand others. Be there for your friends and family, help out those who are in need, put more effort and thought into your words and actions, and watch your confidence grow as a result.

Looking good is nice, but being nice is a zillion times better. Be nice.

You can do it.

Think of the Randy Park book, Thinking For Results.

THE MIRROR

The mirror is an integral part of life, at least in the Western world. Or is it just a tool, into which you quickly glance to see whether your hair is OK, makeup is fine (do you need that much makeup?), nose hairs not protruding, no spinach between your teeth, and your tie is straight?

How much time is needed to look at the person in the mirror?

Does it show reality? Really? From whose perspective? Yours? Are you sure that the value you place on that reflection is representative of true market value?

The mirror only shows you the image of the moment, and the reflection you see is open to interpretation. Who is the interpreter? Only one person: you.

Are you smiling or frowning, optimistic or pessimistic, honest or dishonest, loving or loathing? All of these emotions impact how you interpret the reflection of you.

There is so much more to you than what you see in the mirror. Think of all the components that make up what you are and what you do, what you say and what you think, how you work and share and all of the things that others find so appealing in you. Yet you stare blankly into that damned piece of glass and suffer from what you see, pining, as you wish … it were different. (If only …)

Do you think there are others who would love to have your looks, mobility, opportunities, skills, and capacity? Why are you critical of just one element of you, one facet of the diamond that is the entirety of you, captured in that one reflective image?

Honestly, how can a smaller or bigger nose help? What would happen if your eyes were closer together or further apart? What about your eyebrows — does it matter if they are one continuous line of hair? Should any of that change, what real difference would it make in your life? If the reflection in that moment weighs an out-of-proportion amount when considering the whole you, then you have much more to consider, don't you?

It is certain that your body should be clean and free of odor, clad in clothing that has been washed and recently ironed. No arguments there.

The mirror only provides a one-dimensional, shallow view of you. Get over it! You cannot be anybody else as everyone else is taken. Can you accept that?

If you want to work on yourself, never mind the mirror and work on your skills, knowledge, language, mannerisms, and friendships. Build a life that harnesses your goals and work ethic while increasing your self-confidence and self-worth. Get to love yourself based on work and doing the best you can with what you have.

Once those elements have been built up and polished, then look in the mirror. What you will see in that moment will be totally different and I am sure much more pleasing to your eyes. Remember that the mirror is not the issue. You are the one who controls the view you see in the mirror beyond its one-dimensional image. What the mirror is actually telling you is look at what you convey visually but look further as you are so much more.

Hollywood loves pretty people. But there are plenty of roles for others as well. Depending on ego and plenty of other measurable characteristics, it is not the pretty people who dominate in the movies, or gain respect for their ability to portray the characters they play. It takes skill, competence, confidence and, most importantly, an open mind willing to accept correction.

Now, how about you? Are you playing the character of you in the best way you can? The mirror can't help with that — it only shows the data in the moment and is not up-to-date until the next time you pause in front of it.

Its limitation is simply that it cannot see more than the wrapping of the gift standing before it.

What do you wrap up every day? Are you mindful of the contents in the package of, you?

> *Think of the book by Jon Kabat-Zinn,*
> Wherever You Go, There You Are.

DESTINY (WHAT IS YOURS?)

By definition, destiny and fate follow along the same lines, whereby fate governs actions and destiny is the final result.

What is your destiny today? Is it the same as last week? As you look ahead years down the road of what is your life, what will the end result be? Will you have created the destiny that you set out to create? Will you have applied effort and discipline in such a way so as to impact your life and passage?

You working with you is all about developing your story, a real-life movie that you create every day through your words and actions. Can you see yourself?

Your destiny? Start with a clean sheet of paper, find a quiet space or at least turn off all of the distractions that pollute your silence. Put your name at the top and start by listing the things you want to accomplish in your life. Allow yourself to be creative and go beyond what you have thought before. Disregard your age, financial status and current knowledge.

Being aware that you are in charge of creating your destiny will make your journey far more interesting. It will act as a road map of sorts. You would not just jump into your car and start driving without a map, some money to cover your travel time, rations and maybe accommodations, and ignoring road and weather conditions. Would you?

What are you willing to give up in order to reach your true destiny, the destiny that you desire and for which you are willing to lay it all on the line? What or who is your most formidable obstacle? (Could it be you?)

Richard Morin

Think of the Eagles song, "Take It To The Limit" and, "Time" by Pink Floyd.

There is a line in *Take It To The Limit* where the lead singer, Randy Meisner, says, "I've always been a dreamer, spent my life running round, and it's so hard to change, can't seem to settle down."

In *"Time,"*, the key line for me was, and still is: "And then one day you find, ten years have got behind you, no one told you when to run, you missed the starting gun." This Pink Floyd song still has enormous traction in my life.

Books, seminars, songs, friends ... all using words to convey a message that you can only hear, when you are ready to hear.

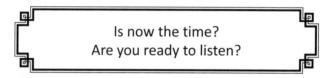

Is now the time?
Are you ready to listen?

Q. What kind of sign are you looking or waiting for?

Q. Whose permission do you seek in order to get to where you want to be?

YOUR PLOT LINE: THE ONE YOU DEVELOP AS YOU WORK THROUGH YOUR LIFE

How is your story developing? Are you on plot? Where are you regarding where you thought you would be at this juncture of your life?

Your history thus far is what it is and not on some linear plane plotted by you and perhaps your parents. More likely, it contains some serious zigs and zags.

Even if you start now — by writing out a complex and detailed plan of where you are going, when you are scheduled to arrive and what you will do when you get there — you will wind up getting it wrong.

Not to worry, though: Life isn't meant to be absolutely perfect. What will your life end up being? Will it be a drama, an action adventure, a sequence of short stories spanning multiple episodes of your life? Will it resemble some form of improv in which everything you do is tied to what others do or say, or some other variation?

You can apply this to your work, the sports you play or any group activity in which what one does or says directly affects others. The most decorated of participants are usually those who are in sync with the moment, capable, flexible, and able to contribute in ways that keep things moving.

The beginning of your life, your story, had little to do with you personally. You arrived in this world and became totally dependent on everyone else. Born on this date, to Mr. and Mrs. Joe Parents and … what else is left to say?

The end is … well, the end. Although we might have some input into when and how this finale will happen, it is abrupt and without an encore. It is the end. So and so died on this particular date. Rest in peace.

But the middle part — yes, the meat in the sandwich, so to speak — is where you get to be creative, to put your own stamp on your own life and where you can be whoever you want to be.

What will your middle part be like? Who will grace the pages of your life's journey? With what sort of conquests will you be credited? How much education or what level of skill will you attain during your tenure? All of this is up to you, so it might be best to reflect from time to time and take stock on your current position, age, earning power, etc., and make adjustments if you believe there is more or a different life ahead of you.

Can you imagine a linear life, where everything is known in advance? You can look at each day and know exactly what the temperature will be, what events will happen, who you will work with, who will be your choice of mate, how much money you will earn, the type of car you will own and when any sicknesses or accidents will strike and knowing how you could prevent those from happening? Boring! How would you ever get motivated? What is it within that straight line of existence that appeals to you?

There have been roughly 87 billion people who have lived before you. And, yes, there are some who will say that they knew exactly what they wanted, did everything they could to go after that goal, and achieved it in the fashion they predicted. But for all of those people, there are billions more who simply lived, did the best they could with what they had, and died.

None of these people asked for cancer, to be shot, to drown or be killed on the road, to fall victim to a storm or be killed by some terrorist. Not one of them asked for that kind of harsh ending, and yet it still happened.

Is it possible to write out a plot or script that consigns life to be a certain way? In my view? No!

It is possible to harness life and do with it what you can while you are here, moment by moment? Yes! But you better be wired, agile and prepared to do whatever it takes when the opportunity arises and with those who accompany that opportunity.

Think of the Valdy song, "Yes I Can."

The camera is rolling, there are no retakes, and no substitutions. What will you do now?

THE JOURNEY; FINDING OR CREATING ONESELF? (OR BOTH?)

Who you are and what you are capable of doing on daily basis has yet to be determined. You might say that you are a certain age or harnessed with a type of disability that limits your options, and all of that will be as true as you want it to be.

But how true is it?

Your life quest is a never-ending one. At each age and stage, you are faced with challenges, resource limitations, physical limitations and many other things that conspire to have you follow a diverging path.

There are youth in the early years of school who find or create their niche in academics or sports and seem to never waver from their initial course. Some would call these people lucky. But if you were to examine their trajectory, you would find that a lot of effort, sweat, practice and mental toughness went into propelling them to where they wound up.

> Pick a destination that appeals to you, and then learn and do what it takes to get there.

The journey continues and the opportunity to find your reason for being here or creating the opportunity you seek is always there. Thinking is required and then choosing, but those are two commodities that are always there for you, as you are a thinking being.

Every journey requires you to stop at various points to check where you are against your intended destination. Are you doing that?

What do you need to complete your journey?

A life of mediocrity is a choice, of course, being defined by events outside of you, and just going with the flow. There is nothing wrong with mediocrity, if you are OK with this particular choice.

Your life, similar to a poker game, provides you with cards. Some people play with the cards they are dealt. Others may take some risky gambles, draw new cards into their hand, and play the odds. What type of poker player are you? How will you be defined, and how do you define yourself?

Think of the Kenny Rogers song, "The Gambler."
("You've got to know when to hold 'em, know when to fold 'em, know when to walk away, ... ")

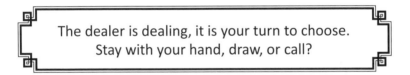
The dealer is dealing, it is your turn to choose.
Stay with your hand, draw, or call?

BEING THE DRIVER IN YOUR LIFE

I have written this in an open format. I am not suggesting anything about you, nor am I claiming anything to be applicable to you or anyone. What I am saying is that in my life, I have experienced much of what I have written and/or have seen elements of this book play out in those who have graced the great stage of what is, and has been, my life.

Some of the work experiences that have contributed to my life included: gas stations, sweeping streets; bartender; on oil rigs, at sawmills, in machine shops, in mints, on construction sites, in underground mines, driving heavy trucks, selling to manufacturers in the United States and Canada, sales companies in Europe, at American military contractors, and car manufacturers. As well, I attended college, was in the air force, police force; I have been running my companies, working with my clients who paid me well to train their upper management and helped develop sales skills in their sales team; I continue to apply psychometric instruments to applicants at my client companies and have learned by doing what I did in raising and watching my children grow.

I have been a passenger as time rolled past, and I have also been the driver, choosing the roads, planning my destinations, dealing with navigation through the various perils I have faced. Given the choice, I much prefer being the driver, and perhaps you will as well.

Of course, being the driver does not mean that you commandeer the entire voyage. It just means that you help steer, help choose destinations, help to make the plans for the voyage, etc. There are many others who will be there to help you on your way, and who make your passage possible.

Once you know yourself, have built up your competence and confidence, are in harmony with how you are made up, your propensities and habits, then you are better able to drive, work with and accomplish tasks and goals with others.

Think of the Don Henley song, "New York Minute."

There is much to do, and we are burning daylight. Let's get on the path of self-determination. You drive.

Why not you?

FOR EVERY MILE OF ROAD, THERE ARE TWO MILES OF DITCH

The roads on which you drive are not very different than the life you live. There are plenty of perils that await you if you are not awake, alert and fixed on your intended destination. There are also ditches that run parallel to the road that is your life. Do you have both hands on the wheel and eyes on the road?

As you navigate your way through your daily life, you will see all kinds of ditches ahead of you. Sometimes you can see in the rear-view mirror that you narrowly missed going into one. Then again, hindsight does not illuminate the road ahead.

The ditches that run parallel to the road you are on take the shape of words you might have used, emotions you could have taken to heart, expressions that may have exacerbated an already strained situation, actions possibly taken, and among everything else, dietary/substance choices you make or avoid.

The analogy of the ditch running alongside the roads of life is a good one. If etched into your mind will keep you agile and fleet of foot as you move along the road that is your life.

How do you wind up in the ditches?

By not doing what others wanted or expected from you, having previously agreed to do so. By doing shoddy work that winds up costing time and money. By not showing up when you said you would. Or, by not sticking with an agreement that you initially made.

The people with whom you live and work and those who oversee you rely on you to perform, and are aware of your capabilities. They can only tolerate so much before they decide to move on and leave you behind. They can only pull you out of the ditch so many times.

Take your health, for instance, both mental and physical. It is your health, and yours to do with as you please.

> A body and mind that are abused do not age as well, compared to a body and mind that are properly managed and maintained.

The ditch is full of different people. Some are lazy, others who know better and can do better but simply choose to do nothing. Some simply took their eyes off the road, missing the turn that would have taken them to a new destination.

Some of these people expect others to carry their load, to pay their bills and to do for them what they are capable of doing themselves. That, of course, is a ditch mentality.

As your journey through what is your life continues, stay out of the ditch.

Think of the Christopher Hitchens book, Mortality.

The Little Engine That Could: Published by Platt and Monk in 1930, first printed in 1920.

This story never gets old. Whether you read it yourself, or to your kids or to your grandparents, the story is as applicable today as it ever was, for everybody.

The story is all about the little train engine designed to haul trains around the rail yard. The larger and more powerful locomotives were used to haul trains across the country.

One day, after all of the big locomotives refused to haul a line of rail cars over a steep incline, the only option was to ask the little engine if he would get it done. He steps up, and hauls the entire long train of rail cars up and over the steep incline saying every inch of the way, "I think I can," "I think I can," I think I can," and once he got over the hump he then said to himself, "I knew I could," "I knew I could," "I knew I could."

The moral of the story is plain to see, but for some reason eludes many on their way through their life, doubting themselves all of the way.

Do you believe in yourself? If so, good! If not, why not?

What, then, is stopping you from getting it done? What are the things you want to get done?

Whether you are in sales, construction, driving long haul trucks, in a professional position, a company president, it doesn't matter. There are always obstacles in your way and you can become derailed in your efforts, looking too long at the task instead of just getting it done.

You just have to think back three or four generations to see the hardships our forbearers had to endure. And yet, they built the cities, roads, factories and the schools you use today. They had large families, worked in the fields, cut wood, dealt with harsh conditions and with no help from the government. There were no unemployment checks, no welfare, and no other money except what they earned.

They had one thing going for them — that was themselves, their belief and their determination to succeed and exceed at life, while knowing that they could do it.

I believe in you. Do you?

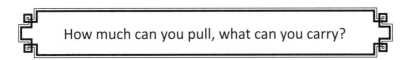

How much can you pull, what can you carry?

What will you do?

Just do it.

Think of the Doug and the Slugs song, "Making It Work."

HAPPINESS

What constitutes a happy life for you? Have you written out what those ingredients contain? If you have not done so, why not start now?

If happiness in all of its facets is not a part of your current life, what is it that needs to change, be adjusted, or achieved in order to make happiness a part of your day, every day? Happiness can only be a part of your day because, let's face it, not everything brings happiness. Dealing with someone over an issue or argument can be stressful; being late for work or a meeting due to traffic will cause you stress; doing some tasks at work can be tedious and boring. But just like a normal day when clouds obscure the sun, it still shines through from time to time and is very enjoyable when it does. Such is happiness.

Of course, there are aspects to your life that give you pleasure. Then there are those other aspects in which you do things out of habit, peer pressure, or whatever which robs you of the joys you could be experiencing.

What are you willing to do to have happiness in greater quantity and over sustained periods? Are you prepared to put aside your need for instant gratification that has led to a herky-jerky life in order to achieve long-term joy?

There are magazines, advertisements, Web sites and the companies that host them who have a lot to gain from mass consumption, and who will have you believe that by losing twenty pounds by using their product or service, you will be happy. Or that if you wear certain clothes, spray yourself with a particular perfume, or consume their products, that all manner of good fortune including friends, lovers etc., will come your way bringing you happiness.

Do these all sound too good to be true? Do they resemble quick fixes that never endure, and that with time will be replaced with more of the same, continuing an endless search for a solution that is truly within you, right now?

Where does happiness come from? Is it from buying something? Owning an article? Living in a certain type of house or apartment in a specific part of town? Are you going to be blissfully pleased forever because you have a phone from the leading supplier? Do you believe that by simply wearing clothes stamped with the name of a celebrity or fashion giant it will have you floating on a cloud of contentment? Are you convinced that by eating and drinking copious quantities of unhealthy food and beverages, it will be worth it if you feel a slight uptick on the happiness scale as you sit with your friends?

By now, you are either very aware, or becoming acutely aware that happiness cannot be purchased. That the little spikes in your enjoyment level are short lived as the item you acquired either gets unpopular quickly, or does not do for you what you anticipated it would. In addition to these is the shock you experience when you get your credit card bill and realize that there is no more room to purchase those things that you hope will lift you higher and help you maintain your altitude. (And the interest you pay each month on your credit card removes any joy you might have enjoyed from a purchase.)

The hopes, needs and dreams of the general public differ greatly from the aspirations of those companies who collectively bombard you with their claims, promises, images, endorsements, and associations as ploys to buy more stuff from them.

Their goals are always more profits, as stated in their mission statements and pushed by the CEO, COO, CFO, CTO and all of the other high-earning executives.

Beyond the "stuff" that clutters your life, what is it that would help you find happiness? Is there some undefined goal that, with some thought, effort, analysis, focus (and some work), might be attainable?

Have you applied effort towards obtaining or accomplishing those things that mean something to you, that are worth having and that will endure throughout your life?

Sit down with a pen and paper, or at your computer or electronic device and start plotting a goal or mission statement for your life. Don't worry about accuracy. This is like taking a cross–country drive, heading to L.A., for instance. If there is a bridge out on Interstates 5, 10, 15, 20, or the coastal highway, you don't abandon your voyage; you simply take a detour and sometimes experience all sorts of new ideas and memories as a result. Such is life.

Go ahead and apply your time and energy towards that goal or goals. Become good at completing tasks and winning at each of the challenges that come your way.

Develop your self-worth and confidence by doing what you want to do instead of following the herd and associating with people who are lost, and are only together because they think it is better than being alone. But honestly … have you ever noticed that nothing gets done when you are doing nothing?

Don't misunderstand me. Being social is very important in your life, but excessive socializing does not lead anywhere, just more socializing.

Happiness is there for all of you. It comes wrapped in a protective layer called work, that thin film can be removed with your effort and consistent application of your ever-developing skills.

Can you see it? Will you step out of the well-worn path you find yourself on?

Think of the song, "Can't Buy Me Love" by The Beatles.

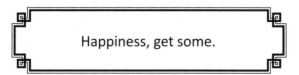

Have you rented a storage unit on the edge of town, used to store all of those things that cluttered your already full life? What will you do with it?

MEDIOCRITY VERSUS GREATNESS

Imagine looking down at your world and seeing all of humanity, walking along in a huge mass, and as is typical and logical of course they are following the great rivers of life, as rivers take the path of least resistance and follow the contour of the earth leading them to the ocean.

Now we are talking about people so let's agree that the ocean is death, and the path they are on, no matter which path only leads to this inevitable destination. (Your future is assured.)

The hordes of people walking along, following those rivers we mentioned are walking in step, following and talking, partying, sharing, and basically moving in-mass.

Some of them dream of doing something more. Others hope to find the gold chest at the end of the next rainbow. A few choose to gamble and buy lottery tickets as a means to get rich quick. Many more may be lost souls who continually seek a better way, but haven't found it yet.

Missing from the herd are the outliers — people who choose to think good thoughts, do smart things, people with discipline and focus who are with others of like mind. You can see these people if you look for them, and if you want you can join them on their difficult journey.

Look up, way up, to the mountains. You will see those few people struggling to climb to the peaks, slipping and falling, scraping their knees and elbows as they fight for every purchase or hand-hold and crevice that can support their weight and move them onto the next outcropping.

Where are they going? They are heading toward their goals, and applying effort to achieve their objectives, in order to enjoy the fruits of their labor later on in life. Besides, the view from the peaks anywhere in life are far more spectacular than what you see in the valleys.

If you feel you want more from your life, are willing to do more, and are tired of following the masses, then start climbing.

Where following the rivers takes you on a long, slow descent, climbing the mountains of life offers you a chance to experience new aspects to life.

The mountain of course is a metaphor as is the path along the river, but both of these are powerful, and you know that the illustration is fitting as the difference between them is glaring. Choosing the mountain path requires a commitment to self and a belief that you can and will make it, risking much on the way.

Each peak can be an education, or a job that seems so engaging, perhaps the learning of a skill or ability, knowing how to play an instrument, or … any of a million reasons to motivate you to the greater heights.

The river path illustration is simple in that it is easy due to the vast percentage of people just following the herd, living day to day, like a hayseed just being blown from this field to the next by the winds of time.

What are you thinking now? Are you feeling challenged and perhaps willing to take a harder look at the path you are on?

Think of the book, Outliers *by Malcolm Gladwell.*
(Being successful as you define it,
depends on many circumstances,
and of course the choices and effort you make)

BETWEEN STIMULUS AND RESPONSE, THERE IS A GAP. LIVE IN THE GAP.

The title of this section, and the choice of words, have been espoused by many a writer and coach or trainer.

Why? Because there is no greater challenge in your life, and no greater return on self-control than the peace and confidence you will enjoy when your pull your own strings, based on real-time events.

Why? Because the wisdom that is yours for the taking resides in the gap between stimulus and response. You are not forced to blurt anything out that you will later regret. There is no need to jump out of just any window if a fire has you trapped on the top floor. There is time to pick the one which is over a large tree or swimming pool.

Living in the gap between all things means being in the moment, present, and aware of your posture relative to the words flowing toward you and the actions being taken by those interacting and intersecting with you.

Remember that nothing is a continuous event. Take music, for example. Without the gaps between guitar riffs, drums, piano, stringed instruments and voices you would be left with a wall of sound that delivers no meaning, no value, no reason to listen or associate with, as it would be simply, noise.

There is peace when you are in the gap because you are making choices in time with the events instead of being suddenly jolted into awareness and making an untimely or inappropriate decision leading to apologies and back peddling a little later on.

Remember that you have a choice when stimulus prompts you. One choice is to do or say something; the other one is to do or say nothing. When you choose to do or say nothing, you are sending a message to the other party or parties that you have thought about the situation and have chosen to let it flow past you, to leave it alone.

> It has been said: "Better to have someone think you are stupid than to open your mouth and remove all doubt."

Take someone who swears, a lot, seemingly without thinking. The truth is, they are not thinking; they are not allowing a gap between what is happening and their response. They are falling into the same old way of speaking, the overused words that in most cases do not suit the moment or help them in any way.

If they were to pause, just for a moment, and reach back into their verbal abilities and knowledge of their particular language they would be able to offer up something more than a rude and simplistic four-letter word. Their self-worth and value to others would change as a result of using the gap between stimulus and response in order to reply in kind, to take the conversation to a different destination instead of the time worn end it usually takes.

> Words, they are there for the using, and there are so many of them to select from.

Do you find you are being rushed all of the time by all of the demands you have allowed to make camp in your life? Just because the phone rings, do you have to run for it? Do you have voicemail? Some person texts you or retweets you and your electronic device makes a sound, beckoning you to attend to it because you think it is important. What happens if you decide to ignore it? Better yet, why not silence the audible whip that usually has you jumping? Will the message still be there in an hour, or later in the day or next week?

Will it matter if you interrupted what you were doing in order to look at some unimportant message? It will matter to the person who wants to maintain his/her connection with you instead of having it broken by the distraction. If you want to show how much you value other people, listen to them and show your appreciation for them through concentration and managing your distractions.

Let's say someone is upset, frustrated or worse yet, enraged with you so much so that you can practically see his/her veins popping, face turning crimson, or hear the harsh edge of their raspy, screaming voice amid the other's angry, insulting diatribe. What would happen if you said nothing? Would you be removing the wood or flammable material from the fire? What would happen to the vengeful person with a large boulder on their shoulder straining to engulf you in their moment of anger and hate, would the steam slowly fade away and leave them embarrassed at their outburst if you simply stood silent, with a bemused look on your face?

If in that gap or moment, you made a choice to not lower yourself to such angry people's levels, to simply step back and let them spew their true nature at you — marveling at the power you have exercised over the situation — would you have learned something about yourself and your importance?

How are you at social situations or conversations whether in a group or in one-on-one situations? Do you find it difficult to enter the conversation, and once in to remain in stride? Do you think it might be because in the past you stumbled upon entry, clumsily hurling out a few words and then watching in horror as they are used in ways you never intended, leaving you to defend some half-baked meaning assigned to what you have said?

One reason for this might be because, in your quest to be liked and to share in the moment, you did not allow yourself to take a moment to consider where the conversation was and if you should contribute anything at that juncture. Perhaps you were waiting for it to change course and go to where you had more to offer. Or you might have stridently overextended yourself, slowly fading away from the conversation and suffering in self-worth for no good reason other than being too rushed, and simply not being kind to yourself.

All day, every day, you are able to step into the gaps that exist in real time between stimulus and response. It is true that some gaps are much narrower while others are wide with no real time pressure, but they are there and it is up to you to think before you make a move or engage verbally.

Peace, real peace, and bliss exist in your hectic and self-burdened world. It has always been there, is there now and will always be there. Make the choice to think and choose instead of leaping at the first idea, response or solution that you see hanging there.

Pavlov's dog you are not. You do not have to salivate when the bell rings, nor respond in a habitual manner each time a particular stimulus occurs.

There are people who go to Tibet at huge expense in order to spend months and years sitting there in a meditative posture, breathing and learning to be in the moment. You may not have that luxury, life for you is 24/7 including a job, debt, kids, school, bosses, relationships, taxes, family … so what are you to do? (Tibet is not right around the corner.)

The answer lies within you. Make a choice to choose your responses, refuse to engage with the pull of all those things that demand your immediate response thereby nullifying their effect on you.

Take a moment now, stop! Whew … Take a breath … Now another, and feel it enter you and leave you. Be aware of your breath, and only your breath. Just sit there, or stand there, for another moment and learn to let go. *Will it matter at the end of the day if you took a moment for you?*

Now when you stand up or move, do so with purpose. Start by cleaning up those things that interfere with what is your life. Rid yourself of all the prompts as best as you can.

Being in the gap does not mean that you do not venture forth. It means that when you decide to scale a vertical rock cliff in the mountains, where even the mountain goats dare not go, you have considered the invitation, took inventory of your abilities, ensured you had the appropriate equipment and knowledge on how to use it, have read the face of the cliff to ensure the smartest way up, and have now made the choice to start the climb.

Others, and perhaps you, might have just started the same climb without preparation. But that is behind you now, isn't it?

Think of the song, "Minute by Minute" by the Doobie Brothers.

Whew … Breathe!

II: THE SPOTLIGHT IS ON YOU

ROLES PLAYED EACH DAY AND THROUGHOUT YOUR LIFE

As you prepare to face each day by deciding what clothing to wear (functional vs. demonstrative; revealing vs. conservative), applying your makeup if needed, putting on various watches or other alternative jewelry (nose rings, ear rings, tongue rings and other body piercings), and pondering whether to expose or hide those tattoos of yours, do you take into consideration how you will play out the roles for which you are dressing, and the impressions you will make?

Does your attire support or detract from the message being conveyed for the day? (Communication isn't just limited to words.)

At what point did you realize that you are actually performing on some form of stage throughout your life and, as such, carry the power and ability to cast yourself in multiple roles?

> Yes, you, are on stage every day, all day. Be mindful of what you do and say.

It doesn't matter whether you are at work, at play, or with your family — the art of a life well lived is to cast yourself in a role that properly suits you, and which you can broaden each time you portray it.

The people who get into acting as far back as high school or in college may have an advantage over you, as they can better adjust to any number of roles regardless of their surroundings and who is watching. The good news is that you have the ability to catch on quickly and enjoy similar accomplishments as you take on new roles and make them yours. Depending on the situations you encounter, you might even develop your own unique take on how to play a particular role.

In terms of workplace roles, let's take a human resources (HR) manager as an example. That person knows what job requirements are expected, the workplace address is fixed, the reporting hierarchy is in place, and, of course, the business attire dress codes likely have been discussed. However, what is left up to the individual who takes on this role may include: how that person interacts, initiates conversations, addresses any number of issues, deals with a variety of employee concerns, negotiates contracts with union heads, and, perhaps, upper management who may not always be flexible with their demands.

The HR manager, therefore, has a lot of autonomy in terms of how he or she dispatches duties, shows some spirit for the job at hand, chooses appropriate language, and listens to understand each employee's concerns. As a result, the culture of the HR manager's company is at stake.

The same can be said for any job or role. You could be a salesman, cook, driver, mechanic, or higher up the corporate ladder as company executive or president. Each of these positions put the onus on the individual in how he or she interprets, and plays out, that particular role.

Think of what roles you will play as you work through the days of your life. Among the endless list of life *roles*, how do you see yourself portraying a husband/wife, parent, coach, student, police officer, driver, cook, house cleaner, gardener, grandparent, or retiree?

Now would be a good time to think what these roles require from you and how to best prepare for them, because how you do in portraying these roles will be up to you. There will, of course, be others in your immediate social circle who will help contribute to your success. But by and large, how you fill these roles will depend on your flexibility and ability to convey the lines and perform the actions as only you are capable of doing.

Throughout your life, remember that no matter how hard you are on yourself, ultimately your role will be judged on its own merits; there is no benefit in comparing one person against another. There are just too many variables to consider.

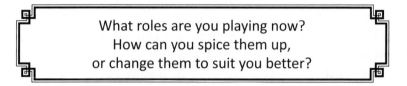

What roles are you playing now?
How can you spice them up,
or change them to suit you better?

Action! Roll cameras — you're on.

Think of the Norah Jones song, "Feelin' The Same Way."

YOU INC.: SELF-DEVELOPMENT USING A SWOT ANALYSIS.

Does your life resemble that of a business?

Well … before you rush to judgment with a resounding "NO," think about it just a little bit (based on your acceptance or denial, it could benefit you):

A business comes alive on a daily basis — even on weekends — and operates with people just like you.

A business is built around a particular skill, product or service. Its success is based on how well the company performs, and that performance has to do with knowledge, delivery, packaging, service, effort, appearance, usage, hours of operation, and much more.

You and I will enjoy success in our lives very closely determined along these lines. People will hire us because of what we know, do, say, act, how much effort we put into our tasks and ourselves, how useful we are, what we are willing to do and will do, how many hours and at what time of day we are willing to perform.

In business and perhaps in life, we can apply what is called a SWOT analysis. This is carried out at various times in a business cycle and is never far from the minds of those who hold power over the company, its profitability and, ideally, its eventual success.

In your life, the view you have of your horizon is not very different. Do you understand money and debt? Do you have skills that will earn you the kind of money you seek? If not, are you willing to do what it takes to learn the proper requirements that will bring in that extra cash? Are you pleasant to work with? Do you fit into the culture of the company with which you aspire to work? What must you do to fit in?

The SWOT analysis is comprised of the following:

- *Strengths:* Well ... what are these strong points that you possess? How can you improve upon your strengths that will benefit you, or make you more acceptable and perhaps more desirable to hire? Once you know your strengths and can focus on defining and enhancing them, your confidence, not to mention your competence, will increase. From there, more good things can happen for you.

- *Weaknesses:* Can you list them? Are you willing to confront those weak points, learn from these and make the necessary improvements? Are you willing to invest the time in order to define and act upon those definitions?

- *Opportunities:* What opportunities are out there for you? Where are they? How are you categorizing those opportunities and based on what criteria? Are you using an old set of strengths or the new, improved strengths identified earlier? Do you focus on your old weaknesses too much or have you moved onward based on an improved you?

- *Threats:* What things are threatening you today? Are they the same threats that have existed for some time and that you have not confronted? What are you doing to highlight those threats, to clarify them for what they really are and how to address them, ignore them, work with them, get help to erase them, or ...?

Summary of SWOT: Life is what it is. Sounds simple to say this, but ... ask yourself what do you want life to provide you. What are you willing to do in order to get from life what you want?

These are appropriate questions to ask, and, in true adult fashion, one should take these into consideration.

A SWOT analysis is not a bad thing to do.

Taking stock of your situation and makeup is an engaging, prudent activity. You can change aspects of your life to produce a more desirable outcome and, ultimately, make life much more rewarding.

You can be a parent, coaching kids, or a manager overseeing a group of employees. You could also be simply a person who realizes that life is happening at every moment, and that it is up to you to play, contribute to your well-being, and engage in as many activities as you like to make this life fun.

You could also be passenger in life, merely going from point A to point B, bouncing from one obstacle to another. Wouldn't you rather take control and navigate away from any potential perils?

Knowing your strengths and weaknesses, and opportunities and threats is critical if you want to be successful.

SWOT ... why not?

Think of the Steppenwolf song, "Born To Be Wild."

YOU WORKING WITH YOU AND OTHERS: THE WORK REQUIRED TO PLAY

Take the new employee who shows up at his/her workplace on Monday morning, early, and prepared to commence what may very well be a long and promising career. He/she has carefully read the employee information packet, printed and signed the requisite forms, and is now inside the new boss's office, ready for the orientation to begin. So far, they made a good first impression, and provided that this new recruit works as well as they can in a spirit of harmony with others, they will be on their way to achieving some personal goals.

This is about you working with you as you make your way through what will be your life. You could be a fresh-faced recruit like that previously mentioned new employee, or you could be a veteran facing each day with a similar perspective. There is always some initial trepidation, or unease, but you can deal with these blips. Of course there will be others with whom you will interact — unless you prefer to be a solitary trapper living in the wild who only deals with the animals you kill and the dogs you take in for companionship. But even the trapper has to emerge once in a while for provisions and also to sell pelts. That, of course, involves conversations, maybe a bit of haggling, but certainly it means learning to get along with others in order to achieve success.

Do you or that lone trapper get better at dealing with people by avoiding them or doing things that require the absence of others? The simple answer is no — but you know that.

> *Think of the Henry David Thoreau book,* Walden. *He may have sought out solitude and was able to remain alone for vast periods of time, but, to what end, could he have achieved more by working with other people?*

People are everywhere. For the hardened trapper, it will just mean that this solitary soul will expedite his trip in order to get back to the peace, not to mention the mosquitoes that await him in the bush, away from other people. But for you, life just keeps on going as you interact with more people and more situations. You are connected and it is the words you use to bridge the gap between you and others that builds relationships of some sort — or not.

The endless daily search for meaning, self, where one fits into the grand scheme of things and alongside others brings us into the far depths of our thinking. Books on this very subject can be of help, as we are often introduced to new thoughts, or ones that continue to resonate with us.

However, some lessons in life can take a long time to learn. Repetition works — you have to thrust yourself into new situations, be open to making mistakes and learning from each episode. Just look at the things you do well and how much effort it had taken to get to this point. Look at how many times you fell down as you learned how to walk; how you mumbled, grunted and raved in ways that nobody could understand as you mastered your language; the number of times that a teacher was on you as you struggled to play your musical instrument; or had you wondering why that coach kept picking on you as you learned the skills of your sport of choice.

Your ability and willingness to work is critical to your success. Although it is fun to play, it just will not get you to where you want to go. With time, experience and perspective, you will find contentment and joy in the various roles you take on, in concert with others. Even though it will be fun, underneath the pleasure you will see that work lies there, and is the basis of all things.

Although TV shows and movies might have portrayed a life of leisure that may be yours for the taking, they lied.

Even musicians who "play" music put in a lot of work to get to the point where they play well with others, and get paid for it. Though they represent part of a band, there is always pressure to learn new songs, to apply their instruments and voices in new ways. Behind all of this is the knowledge that time is not on their side, that the exit is not that far away from the stage where they stand, and that the best time to play well with others and earn what they can earn is now. (The time is always now.)

The same can be said for golfers as well as the professional athletes in tennis, football, baseball, hockey and more. All of these "players" fought hard and worked even harder to get to where they are now, and did so in the face of immense competition.

So, back to you. What kind of work do you want to do, which will reap the kinds of financial rewards you desire? What do you have to learn? How much preparation is involved? What kinds of investments are required, and ... how much work do they entail? (Did I say work again? Tsk, tsk!)

Every day offers a new opportunity to start again, to learn from the past and to move on.

Alcoholics Anonymous has it right, and its maxim is worth remembering each day: Life is a "one day at a time" event; there is a new day every day, and that day is there for us to apply ourselves in the way we choose. (The devil is in the choosing.) It does recovering alcoholics little good to dwell on bad choices, and all of the pain and suffering these individuals have brought upon themselves and others. (Hanging onto pain is, well, painful.)

Instead, AA treats recovering alcoholics as humans who are allowed to have another chance to improve themselves as they redirect their lives along a better, more fulfilling chosen path.

Tiger Woods said it best: ninety percent is what you do next, ten percent is what you did. This from the golf master who could drive a ball into the worst possible locations and then, with whatever club he chose to use, was able to successfully hit that same ball back out and into play.

As you learn how to handle and accept yourself, as well as your unique appearance and abilities, it becomes a lot easier and more pleasant to be productive with, and alongside, others.

The truth and beauty of life is that it keeps us on our toes every day because … every day is different, each situation is unique, and the people who drift in and out of our lives are always in flux themselves leading to exchanges that you cannot predict. They are also evolving.

Think of the John Fogerty song, "Centerfield."

What challenge will you select to work on today?

HARMONY, AS A RESULT OF BEING ABLE TO WORK WITH YOURSELF AND OTHERS

We all love a good song where the voice and instruments come together to form a listening experience that crystallizes our thinking and sways our moods.

We also applaud sports teams and athletes who collaborate to produce a winner against all manner of obstacles and contenders.

We marvel at the companies that invest, recruit, and perform in their sectors producing profit and growth over long periods of time and to great acclaim. Some people in these companies just seem to get along, be in the right place at the right time, and appear to enjoy their time at work.

What about us? Are we harmonizing with our environments, those people who share our lives, the business opportunities that reside within our grasp? Are we adding to the moment and our opportunities? Or are we viewed as liabilities?

You hear people say that someone (say, Bill, Sue, or Mike) is "their own worst enemy." How and why would they say that? Is it true? How can a person be one's own worst enemy?

Being in harmony means fitting in at the right time, in the right way, in each moment as we continue our relentless forward movement.

I say forward movement because there is no going back — and standing still is not an option. So we are always dealing with moments as they arise, whether or not we are ready for them.

In your work life, whether in a school, office, factory, assembly line, transportation sector, mining, oil field, garage, hospital … it is always up to you to step up and do that thing that is needed, and to communicate with others regarding issues and opportunities in a proactive way.

A football player, for instance, must understand the play, see the position of his teammates, be aware of the defensive scheme the opposing team employs, and then leave his mark on the play.

In hockey, there exists a statistic called plus-minus. The plus-side number means how often a player is on the ice when his team's goals are scored; the minus refers to how often said player is on the ice when goals are scored against his team. Over time, this measurement is quite accurate, as the better players' numbers are in the plus category.

Being in harmony means to have the right attitude and willingness, coupled with ability and knowledge that affords you the opportunity to make a difference in your life and that of others. Being in the moment is the challenge of the day, month and life, as it is a moment-to-moment potential. I say potential because there are so many obstacles to "being in the moment," including those we invite into our minds and lives, which may include music, the news, texting, TV, food and much more.

How does it feel to be in the moment? Have you ever had the experience of just being there, in the moment where you are, with the people in that moment or even by yourself where you are aware of all things around you but remain in a state of neutrality? In a non-judgmental way?

Have you experienced the bliss of present-moment awareness and connectivity? Do you want to experience this?

We can talk about meditation later. It does not take much effort, but delivers a nice reward.

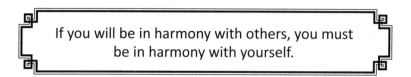

It can take a lifetime to develop a good relationship with the self, but it is worth the effort.

What is there to love about you? List those things that make you the sort of person others want to be with. The list you just created is not static, you can add to it over your lifetime.

Think of the Journey song, "Be Good To Yourself."

You? Yes you, smile at life, it will smile back.

ALL BUSINESS IS PEOPLE BUSINESS

We are all in the people business, because everything is done for, and with, other people. Though this statement is a no-brainer, it is surprising to see how many of us do a poor job at dealing with other people. Often, we may find ourselves complaining that other people won't listen, they're rude, pushy, refuse to collaborate, don't take in others' ideas or opinions into account and generally make our lives incredibly difficult. Reciprocation is always at play, and most of us can only take so much before we react to perceived abuse or just walk away, which can lead to more difficult issues.

If you want to influence others, you require a clear purpose, sound knowledge on what you are getting across, and plenty of patience as you offer up ideas, discuss, listen and explain what you are saying and why.

Influencers are very good at communication, listening and then taking the subject forward in a way that is non-threatening, and, by their calm delivery, actually inviting others into the conversation or situation.

Being a manager/coach/leader can be a great experience, especially if you know how to influence others. Although you may be in an office or warehouse or plant, when you become a manager your job changes in more ways than first apparent. The position requires you to achieve an objective, get work done in an efficient fashion, and do so safely and in a spirit of cooperation with and through those who you are in charge of.

Even though you might be very good at being that leader, there will be times when you scratch your head in disbelief at how things can change so rapidly due to one of your team member's efforts or lack thereof and the effect they have on the rest of the team. These are the times when you will rely on your ability to communicate, explain, motivate and be the leader you are capable of. It is not easy and perhaps getting harder as our society changes.

In business, you are always building a case, developing a new product, approaching a new market sector, and shuffling players on and off your team projects. In life, we use business-like acumen in analyzing whether to invest in new flooring for the house, and pouring over the best deals for that new car purchase or vacation getaway. Your scales get used every day. Sometimes you just have to build a case that might lead you to leave someone, or fire them. (Amounts to about the same thing.)

There are people who focus on process or technology, systems and machines, drawings and details. While lost in a sea of technicalities, these specialists may not often deal with the people for whom they work, or be in contact with those who will use, buy and deal with the very things they are working on. This might bode well for them, providing they recognize their solitary pursuits, and hire someone else to deal with their users and customers.

But ... eventually these same technocrats will have to deal with people in some way, shape, or fashion. If they have backed away from every human challenge that came at them, they will suffer as they try to work through issues where emotion and feelings are running hot.

Turning away from challenging situations is simply a bad strategy as it only hurts you in the short- and long-term. Soon your response to any threat from people is to either clam up, walk away or simply slip deep into yourself, hiding from what could be a good lesson and a promising relationship with the person in question.

> It might be OK for a child to hide behind his mother's skirt, but unless you face up to the challenges that people offer up to you every day, you will remain a person who shies away from conflict and remains in your own shadow.

What is the worst thing that can happen to you when you stand up, and have a direct exchange with someone from whom up to now you have hidden?

Well … they might start with a "hello" to which you can reply, "Hello and good morning" to which they can then return to you with, "What can I do for you today?" and … you then have all of the options in the world at your disposal. Think about it: Most likely they have moved on from any indiscretions you fear they remember and might harbor. Most people simply forgive and forget, giving others a second chance. (Do you?)

At the end of this first conversation, you can conclude with a follow-up plan to speak again, or have a coffee, or share a favorite book if that entered into your conversation. Or you can ask for advice if they are a person in the know, or inquire if they are planning to attend a particular function. The options are limitless.

The key here is that once you break the ice, and then see that person again, they will no longer be the person they once were in your mind. They will now be an acquaintance with whom you can share a hello, a brief exchange, or whatever.

Take the bricks, steel, windows and technology out of a company or building, and what is left? People!

Yes, people, they are everywhere.

Can you think of someone you have once skirted, and now you need to face? Who?

Think of the book, The Starbucks Experience
by Joseph A. Michelli

FIRST IMPRESSION / LAST IMPRESSION

Preparing for that all-important first encounter with another individual or group can be nerve-wracking, and some of that anxiousness might sometimes be deserved. But for the most part, there is no reason to feel anxious or nervous about having the chance to make a first impression. If you have the opportunity to do so, you will get to meet new people, expand your horizons and let others know who you are, what you are and what you can do. All this is a good thing and should be met with great enthusiasm.

Take a job interview, for example. Before going in, you shower, shave or put on makeup, do your hair just so, dress to impress, sharpen your memory on key subjects that may come up, and memorize your resumé so that you don't get caught in a lie or exaggeration. Most importantly, you prepare to arrive on time for your interview.

Now, unless this was the first time you showered and shaved, spiffed up your features with makeup, wore nice clothing, were punctual, and read applicable material relative to your area of expertise, what else do you have to worry about? If your resumé is based on your true history without containing any elaborations or added colour, and you are applying for a position that you are confident you can perform, there should be no other need to be concerned or in a panic. (You see, worry has no place in this situation.)

The problem is that people knock themselves out when going for an interview, but what they fail to realize is that it is not the first impression they have to worry about. It is the last impression that will stay with the interviewer, who might now be their new boss.

The same applies with first dates. If you are a charlatan, going way out of your comfort zone to make this great first impression, what do you think will happen after the tenth, or hundredth encounter, if in fact they did not see through your guise and already deserted you based on some fictional performance you gave?

If you are comfortable with being yourself, living as you do, working at the jobs you have held, and socializing with your usual crowd, then carry on. It's best to be honest with yourself and with others rather than build some elaborate façade that others will ultimately see through.

Abraham Lincoln once said, "You can fool some of the people some of the time, but you can't fool all of the people all of the time." Why would you like to fool someone anyway? Imagine if you have sold someone a fraudulent bill of goods concerning yourself and your abilities? Can you live with the thought — that you purposely lied to someone else?

If you want to change your circumstances and live an entirely different life, then do the work necessary that will make it happen. Don't worry about getting a better job or meeting someone who differs from your current crop of friends or social acquaintances. When you learn to do the things that the new job requires, or enjoy living the way the people you want to be with live, it will happen for you. Keep learning as you go.

In other words, when you learn what you need to know in order to support the first impression you will make, success will be yours based on your ability to perform — now and in your future.

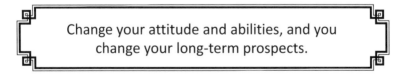

Change your attitude and abilities, and you change your long-term prospects.

MANAGERS, COACHES, LEADERS AND PARENTS

If you are a manager, coach, leader, parent, or someone who influences others, or if you aspire to do any of these things well, you will find some good material within these covers that will help those you work with and train, to see themselves in the guiding light you are providing.

In your role as a coach, team member, leader, parent, partner, business owner or manager, how you work with others requires both an objective view of yourself and the people with whom you are engaged in order to help them from where they are now to the level you believe they can achieve, maybe even exceed.

It is not enough for you to just believe in others. It is critical for them to not only have faith in themselves and their abilities, but also to see that, by consistently putting in the effort, others can vastly improve their abilities and knowledge. Some would define this as work.

Your job, in part, is to cut though the noise in their heads and reach a point where they see the light you are putting in front of them and to take that illuminated path in a spirit of trust.

This trust will partly come from the bond you build based on how you understand your group. Although they are a part of your family, company or a team, you see how they are not exactly the same as their teammates, and you treat them accordingly.

Any coach will tell you that coaching is a mental game. It requires insight into the people who make up the team, and allows the coach to know how to goad that team into a daily regimen of repetition, review, analysis, examination, measurement, and then correction.

Growth may be slow at times, and some people on your team may be inclined to ignore your guidance, depending on distractions and other influences. It takes a consistent tone and firm guiding hand that other people need to accept in order to achieve their potentials.

Your job is to help them see it when they believe it, versus believing it when they see it. They need to see themselves as the person they can truly be, rather than being like the ones who only believe anything when they see it.

What you are instilling in your group members is the belief that they have a gift that you and they are going to release. Think of how a sculptor works. He or she slowly chips away the granite, one hammer and chisel blow at a time, eventually exposing — and then freeing — the encased figure.

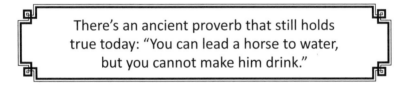

There's an ancient proverb that still holds true today: "You can lead a horse to water, but you cannot make him drink."

Being a coach, leader or parent requires patience, coupled with faith and belief applied consistently, and is a skill that develops over time the more it is used.

Stay with those people you are coaching, be patient, and soon enough they will lift their heads and do what you are coaching them to do. Success will come once you have established the necessary connection.

Is it the fault of children, potential athletes, musicians, or students if they fail to live up to their potential? That's tough to answer, but it is certain that chemistry between them and their mentors plays a big role — perhaps more than you think.

Coaches get fired all the time. Why? It could be for many reasons: their lack of competence, their ability to communicate, or perhaps they never developed a base of trust from which they could motivate and relate to their subjects and now their words have fallen on deaf ears, who knows for sure? The relating thing is huge, though. Just look at your own experiences: who were the mentors who motivated you into doing something new or different? Ask any fired coach what he/she learned from being let go, and he/she will tell you they learned a lot about people, if that's their honest answer.

In the case of a parent, the negative consequences are greater for both the child and the parent as the impact of the parenting can last a lifetime. Leading, training and developing others is a noble activity and one that is highly regarded. My hope is that you will see the requisite skills and propensities within yourself and apply them the best way you can, while learning as you go. The world, and some aspiring and as yet unidentified talent is waiting for you, and importantly what you can do with them as they struggle to be free of the granite that encases them.

Think of the song, "Wearing the Inside Out" by Pink Floyd.

Think of some of the influencers in your life, coaches or otherwise. If you need one, find one.

Being led is one thing; leading others has more to it than just holding the light.

MENTOR

This book can be a quasi-mentor to you. Like all good mentors, it will not provide you with "the answer" to your query or problem but will help you to find your way, through thinking, reflecting and digging into yourself to seek what best fits you and what you want to achieve.

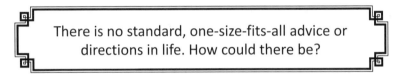

There is no standard, one-size-fits-all advice or directions in life. How could there be?

Like all unwanted advice, it can amount to, or lead to, nothing. Then again, you could follow this old Buddhist saying: "When the student is ready, the teacher will appear." Perhaps by you reading this book, it signals a readiness to examine your life, and perhaps make some adjustments.

Do you take time to sit, reflect and examine the choices in front of you and all the various possible outcomes? Snap, hasty decisions can lead to tears, regret and lost time.

Who do you look up to as you work through untangling the kinks in your life? Do you have someone who is there for you, offering sage advice and guidance, as you make decisions and choose directions from the myriad options you face each day? What are you learning from this mentor?

Do you have a hero from the movies, or perhaps someone who wrote an autobiography that reveals what the book's subject endures as he/she became the finished product we see. (Remember the mirror, and that what you see is not the whole picture.)

I would like you to consider being a mentor at some point in your life. When you ask those chosen to be mentors, you will hear from them and the people they mentored how rewarding the process can be.

When you read about the great successes in life, you will often come across mentions of specific individuals to whom successful people owe a debt of gratitude for their great accomplishments.

Successful people may talk in general terms about some teachers, parents, perhaps coaches, who have helped them get to where they are today. Yet they will also hone in on a select individual or two who went beyond mere coaching and offered adult advice; it's here where you will see or hear the word mentor. (Does the Star Wars character Yoda come to mind?)

The mentor does not "tell" the mentee what to do. Instead, the mentor points out the results of some recent action or future issue, discusses all available options, and lets the mentee head off and do the best he/she can, now armed with one more pearl of wisdom.

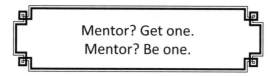

Mentor? Get one.
Mentor? Be one.

Think of the book, Losing my Virginity *by Richard Branson.*

LISTEN, SEEK TO UNDERSTAND

Perhaps one of the hardest lessons to learn is how to listen. With two ears and one mouth one would think it should be easy, but ... alas, it isn't.

To make this easier to comprehend, let's break down the act of listening into three sections:

1. Mentally prepare to listen by putting aside concerns and worries. If you do not have the time in that moment to listen properly, tell the other person, and either make time or invite them to return when you can pay proper attention to them.

2. Capture the message by listening first, taking notes if necessary, ask questions that enhance the flow coming from the speaker in order to truly understand what they are wanting to convey.

3. You may like the sound of your voice, but this isn't the time to verbally hog the limelight. Eliminate distractions and take a breath before you even think of interrupting the speaker. Actively listen to fully understand the person doing the speaking before you rapidly chime in and expect others to understand you.

Oddly, we learn how to present, speak in public, put on presentations, and yet, there is no attention paid to the art of listening.

When you think of how you learned up to now, it involved a lot of listening. In school, you get to sit for hours listening and then get tested on what you just heard.

Once you graduate from school and stop taking courses, you somehow fall into the role of speaker, and seem to stop learning as a result.

Try listening more, and you will be surprised at how much more there is to this world.

Hello? Are you listening? Really?

> *Think of the book,* The Seven Habits of Highly Effective People *by Stephen Covey.*

DEALING WITH ISSUES

We all face issues, all of the time. How do you deal with them? Do you think? Delay? Pass these off to someone else? Deny? Or simply get started?

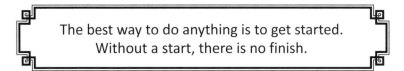

The best way to do anything is to get started.
Without a start, there is no finish.

Begin by putting the issue at hand in perspective. Will it result in your death or the death of others? Will it bankrupt you? Will it tarnish your image irreparably? Will it result in the loss of your job, or your hair? Will it affect your health? What is the worst-case scenario that may result from this issue?

Really? That's it? So why worry?

Now you have a better idea of the issue's magnitude, and can then put a plan in place. Perhaps ask for advice from a mentor or someone you trust, and take the next step in addressing it.

Most, if not all, issues stem from, or have something to do with, people. I know this sounds like one of those "duh" statements. But if the problem is with people (of which you are one), then solving and dealing with issues should not be as vexing as it is — at least in your mind.

When dealing with problems, issues and such, you need to remove the person or people from the equation. Once you have done this, you now have the gist of the problem — as you see it.

As an example:

- You are all dressed up in your best attire, going to a momentous event on the other side of town.

- On the way to this function, you are to pick up your boss, who you happen to have a crush on.

- You call for a cab, go through all of the voice prompts, finally get someone on the phone, but there is a language barrier and after much repetition and spelling out of words, you get across your need and the cab is dispatched.

- The clock ticks forward, closing in on the time when you ought to be in your boss's driveway and then off to your destination.

- Time is pressing, bearing down a high level of pressure on you. You call the cab company to verify that the cab is on its way, and to ensure they have the correct address.

- When your call finally clears all of the voice prompts and you get someone on the line, there is again a language barrier which only adds to your sweat-induced anxiety, a lot.

- That sweat has penetrated your best clothing, and you have large half circles of drenched material hanging from your armpits; your makeup is starting to smear and your hair is losing its bounce. In short, you look like you have just fallen into a swimming pool.

- You are frantic now, biting your nails, cursing in a way that would make construction workers blush, and you are pacing, fast, which produces even larger volumes of salty sweat.

- In your mind, you have descended into the depths of depravity, thinking of all the things you are going to tell this #%^$#&*$*#&%*#& cabbie, and how he will feel your anger like lashes on the back of a thief.

- You look outside and there appears your cab, and the driver happens to be looking your way, beckoning you.

- You are now late to pick up your boss, and even later to arrive at the event, really late.

- You grab your coat and run out the door, (not realizing that your keys remain in the alcove on the table beside your wallet or purse, which also contains your cellphone, boss's address and credit cards).

- You are now trotting down the driveway, in a rage, eyes squinting with hate as you look for vengeance and a chance to hurt this person who has made you late.

- The cab driver is out of the car now. You see a huge man with bulging biceps and massive hands holding the door for you. He has a broad smile and, as he motions for you with a sweeping gesture to enter the car, he says in a deep, resonating voice, "Good evening, it is such a pleasant night."

What do you say to your cab driver?

- As it turns out, there was an accident, and subsequent power failure in the middle of town, all the traffic lights were not functioning, ambulances and fire trucks clogged the intersections, and this poor man was trapped, like a big bear in a trap, unable to move. He asks for forgiveness and displays great remorse for being late.

- The problem was not him and now you feel awful, burdened with guilt, and shame at how quickly and unjustly you can turn against another human being.

- You now become aware that you don't have your wallet or purse, and as you are about to ask the cabbie to wait (irony) while you retrieve this wallet or purse, you have a vision of where it is, alongside your keys and worst of all, you cannot even call your boss on your phone.

- So you ask the cabbie if you can borrow his phone, your boss reluctantly answers as he/she does not recognize the caller, and you let him/her know that you are on your way, and as a footnote, you ask if he/she can pay for the cab.

What can you take away from this issue?

- Stuff happens, all of the time. What's important is how you deal with the unexpected stuff; this will make you what you are or what you can become.

- Listen to other people, give them their due, allow yourself to understand instead of always wanting to be understood.

Situations happen all day, every day in your life. Inject some humour into the situation, separate the person or people from the event, and then address the core issue or result in question.

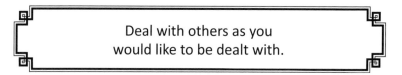

Deal with others as you would like to be dealt with.

Think of the book, The Seven Spiritual Laws of Success *by Deepak Chopra.*

POPULARITY

The best, most slimy, gooey, lying, cheating, self-absorbed, narcissistic, promise-making politician/ lawyer might obtain 70 percent of the popular vote — that is, if he shakes hands with everyone, hugs every grandmother, and kisses every baby.

The popular vote is not the same as popularity, and most of us might hit the 50 percent mark in terms of how popular we are with others.

Now how about you? The question is, why do you want to be loved and adored by everyone? What good would it do you, and for how long will they have that particular feeling for you before you say or do something that changes their mind?

If you are a supervisor, in charge of production of any kind through the effort of others, you might want to be popular and liked. But in that supervisory role, your job is about keeping the production moving along, with help from people who work under your tutelage. Some will like you, others won't like you. Some people may even have utter hatred for you. Are you OK with all that?

The boss will find it impossible to be popular and be friends with everyone. It is ill-advised to go that route. Instead, strive to be friendly at your workplace, while earning your wage and producing results to expected levels.

You need to have some good friends who like you for what you do and say on a consistent basis — in fact, they probably appreciate your wit and charm and like being with you. But within the workplace, it's a big mistake for supervisors to use the word "friend," as opposed to "friendly." when engaging with your work teams.

Popularity is sought after, but genuine popularity is hard-earned and in most cases fleeting for those who use too broad a brush.

Given the choice, would you prefer to be broadly popular or maintain a few close, and deep, friendships?

Be friendly. It is fun. If things line up, true friendship can be a result.

Think of the song, "Crazy as Me" by Alison Krauss.

INSTANT GRATIFICATION

Have you ever watched a young child acting badly because they want "everything" now? Their face is contorted. They are screaming and being bullish with a big bottom lip while doing everything to ensure they get all of the attention from those adults in the room.

Not pretty is it? What is it with some children, or you might more accurately ask, what is it with the parents of these children?

Why did the parents give in to every demand so that the child begins to believe they are entitled, and these poor parents who should know better just keep giving in and saying yes to every demand? Who suffers the most in these relationships, the parents might look worse for wear in the short term, but over time it is the child who suffers longer and in more disturbing ways as they grow older and enter the real world, the one where mommy and daddy are not there to provide for them.

What about you? Do you act badly because things did not come to you the way you wanted them, when you wanted them?

The urge/demand/habit of wanting everything now is a powerful force that frequently works against you. Through your inability to be in the moment, to be in harmony with what is currently forming your reality, you hurt yourself in ways that are hard to overcome, and contribute to your issues.

For those of us living in a Western society, where practically everything revolves about consumption, life is an endless train speeding along a track built by those who benefit the most from our false belief that what they say is important.

This can include companies, religions, government, our kids and significant other and a whole host of competing interests, competing for your heart, soul and of course, money.

The storage companies endorse the "have everything now" mentality, they just keep building rows and rows of storage units that just keep filling up with stuff, most of which never gets used.

This is why you need to carve out some time for you, in order for you to connect with yourself and to listen to your core being who has a message for you:

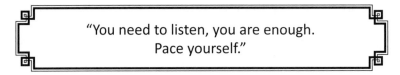

"You need to listen, you are enough. Pace yourself."

If instant gratification led to peace then it might be a good thing. But as best as I can see it is a habit that leads to a continual strain on resources, relationships, countries, employees and employers, children and everyone else we come into contact with.

What is this ever-powerful urge to have everything, NOW? How did it get so strong within our psyche?

There is a gapping difference between having goals and earning just rewards, versus demanding everything, NOW!

Think of the song, "A Man For All Seasons" by Al Stewart.

DO YOUR JOB.
(THIS MIGHT HAVE BEEN THE
TITLE OF THE BOOK, BUT …)

Bill Belichick, the much-celebrated coach of the NFL's New England Patriots, uses many play schemes, training methods and communication tools and has assistant coaches to help with everything from strength training, nutrition, critical thinking and much more.

Belichick's message is simple. He wants people to be aware of the big picture, and those around them, but he wants them to focus on one thing, more than anything, themselves. The three words most associated with him are these: Do your job.

In his words, if everyone does their job to the best of their ability, good things will happen. They will win more than they lose, they will score more points, stuff the opposing offence, and have a much better time during the game. His message contained within those three words is that although winning might not be everything, it is much more desirable than loosing.

If you do your jobs, the way they can be done, every day, there will be no need for regret or pining for the lost opportunities that slipped through your fingers. Tears of regret will not displace the joy of a job well done, and the feeling of confidence from doing so.

Think of all of the jobs you do, from student, sibling, friend, employee, employer, father, mother, brother, sister, grandchild, grandparent, all the way through your life, how would you rank yourself at those jobs?

Most of the problems we all face are based on either us or someone simply not doing their jobs, the way the job should be done. Know what makes up each job you do through the day, stop and make sure you understand how to do what it is you are asked to do.

Before people get married, it would benefit them both if they sat down and listed all of the tasks each will be expected to do, responsibilities that have to be accepted, and roles each will play. This list or understanding needs to be created over time, as there is too much at stake for haste to create a tragic ending. Expected is a key word here, because without clear communication, expectations go un-fulfilled and friction commences to really heat up the relationship, and not in a pleasurable way! The divorce rate is due in part to people simply not doing their respective jobs, or doing their job in a way that the partner had not envisioned, and that both had not articulated.

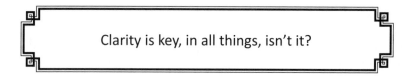

Clarity is key, in all things, isn't it?

Jobs and job descriptions are the same; too much detail will tie a person up. On the other hand, if someone is to earn the money they expect, there needs to be clarity and regular discussions to ensure both sides agree with behaviour and results.

Coaching and being coached are integral parts of life. You may not like to be coached, but … how else will you improve? Your mother loves you as you are, but your coach / manager / spouse / … wants you to be more. They both see it.

Mediocrity is easy to achieve. Just go through motions and never take a hard look at yourself, dismiss suggestions offered to you and ignore the warning signs. You might have fun for a while, but the results will be plain to see and your tenure at work or in relationships will be short-lived.

Those who play (work) for the Patriots are expected to watch hours and hours of film in order to see where they fit into the plays and where they missed their assignments. The onus is on them to take self- development seriously, every day, doing the work that it takes in order to play for the New England Patriots, and get the occasional nod from Bill Belichick. (Maybe even a smile.)

What job, or what part of your jobs are you working to improve on now?

Think of the song, "Getting Better" by The Beatles.

Doing your jobs in life, is life.

PRODUCTIVITY/WORK ETHIC

Out of all the things you can influence directly, your personal productivity and work ethic are two of the most important. The good news is that the ball is entirely in your court relative to how productive you are and what kind of work ethic you possess, and employ. (Can do — will do.)

It is important to consider how you apply yourself in your life, and depending on what you will admit to, perhaps have a little talk with yourself about your attitude and how what you think affects your output, and those around you. It is not all about you, and what you do, or don't — certainly you play the leading role in your life. It also has to do with how you are with others, how you communicate, share, pick up the slack, step forward, volunteer, listen, understand, contribute, and much more.

Your ability to take on tasks and complete them in a timely manner with and through others will determine the kind of life you will build around yourself. There are those who go through life saying that they are going to work smart and not hard. But let's not fool ourselves; you might have a very detailed plan to build a house or business, but somewhere in those plans, and probably hovering over them like a large cloud is something called work.

This includes the work required to earn the money to get the plans developed and then construct the house, and the work you will invest in decorating and furnishing the house, then the work needed to landscape your new yard, and so much more unless you have worked hard enough leading to enough earnings and savings to pay someone to do all of these things. (How do you get rich? Work. How do you stay rich? Keep working!)

Productivity and work ethic determines how you do in school based on learning through repetition and studying. Later on, when you get your first job it will determine how long you keep that job, whether you enjoy it based on self-appreciation, and whether you are valued by your employer — which can then lead to promotions and other opportunities.

Is it possible that you can ramp up your productivity and work ethic? Yes it is. Almost as easy as tuning in your radio to your favorite channel, WIIFM! (What's In It For me.) How do you accomplish this goal of dialling up your ability to get more done with the time and resources allocated to you in this life?

You start now. Today. Approach the next thing with a clear intent to finish what you started, without interruption or delay. This could be writing the next memo or email, making that phone call that you have dreaded making all day and delaying what you think will be the onset of pain as a result of making that call, or perhaps it is cutting the lawn, painting that room that has needed it for some time, washing those dishes that keep piling up, or any number of things that often take way too long to complete. What am I saying here? You have to start at some point and put some oomph into your effort.

Productivity/work ethic are habits learned or not at an early age. Later on in life, you can be influenced in much the same way that your parents or guardians influenced you, in part through books, listening and seeing value in the leaders of the companies you work for, successful friends, movies, biographies and much more.

Like anything in life, there has to be a need in order for you to reach up to the next branch. As a child, that need is to be loved and to feel a part of the family that leads you to do more and mimic those adults on your horizon. The need later in life comes from seeing there is more to life than what you have; by doing more you can have more.

The question is, who has their hand on the switch that turns your body and mind on or off? You! What is it that freezes your actions such that you remain turned off, in too low a setting, or in the middle between action and inaction?

The problem is usually not in being too productive or working too hard. It mostly lies on the other end of the spectrum with people doing far less than they are capable of and therefore missing vast parts of the life that was theirs all along, simply by doing the work.

WIIFM? Tune in and turn up the volume.

Think of the song, "Where Corn Don't Grow" by Travis Tritt.

What will you do now? Write a goal you have been thinking about?

QUALITY

You are sitting in a restaurant about to eat some desirable dish, or in a store about to plunk down your hard-earned cash on a particular item for which you have been saving up to purchase, or paying someone to perform a task such as painting your house, fixing your computer or baby-sitting your kids. In each of these scenarios, quality matters.

The same can be said about the work you do on the job, or how you make your bed, build a sandwich, shovel the driveway, mow the lawn or spend time with someone.

You expect quality and you might put up with less, but if you have to put up with a lesser quality effort and results, you will undoubtedly not return for the same experience. By developing your eye for quality, and applying yourself in all things you do through focus and discipline, the rewards will be almost endless.

This old saying holds true: "If you don't take the time to do it right the first time, when will you have time to do it again a second time?" It is a tune that is always playing.

As you look at your life and see the results of the things you have done, can you see where perhaps quality might have been short changed for haste, distractions or lack of concern?

Just as you trust the bridge-builders on whose structures you drive each day, or the airplane builders whose crafts soar through the skies above, we also trust you to work in a conscientious fashion with a solid and quality result that we have faith in.

If you let others off with shoddy workmanship, what does that say about you? The same is true in reverse, it is your choice to get it right, each and every time and although mistakes can and do happen, these mistakes are easily forgiven if you know the person put all their might into the task, and have learned along the way.

What areas of your life will you apply more effort in order to have a quality result? What can you start doing better in order to commence building a legacy of quality results?

Think of the song "Friends In Low Places" by Garth Brooks.

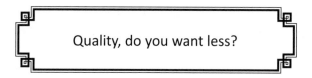

What areas of your job or life will you apply more effort?

EXPERIENCE?

When you hear someone say they have five, ten or twenty or more years of experience at a particular job or skill, what do they mean?

Did they learn a skill twenty years ago and have been applying the same technique the same way for twenty years, in other words, one year of experience applied twenty times? Or, within that twenty-year span did they upgrade their knowledge, learn new methods, tap into shortcuts, and develop new and better ways of getting it done?

What if, when you are speaking with a prospective employer, a team or band you wish to join, or even another person with whom you want pursue a long-term relationship, you had them all understand how much your experience will help make these unions successful?

What if the company with whom you interviewed understood that you can handle interpersonal issues, conflict, recalcitrant people, and can further contribute to its profitability because of your past experience?

If the team you want to join knew that you had the perseverance, the strength of character and the vision to contribute in a big way based on proven experience, would they look at you differently?

The band might show more excitement in you had they realized you possess the maturity to deal with life on the road, and the discipline to rehearse however long it takes to tighten up the group's sound.

That male or female whom you desire for that long-term relationship might fall for you even faster if they understood what you have been through and how those experiences have honed your capacity for love, your desire to help in keeping the house neat and clean, paying down the debts, cooking, making love, and as a supportive parent who knows how to raise children.

So take stock of your experience. Be comfortable explaining to people that you know what you are doing, and that you believe in your abilities. Have them visualize you in their presence and how there would be a good fit based on you, being you.

Experience comes from thrusting yourself into all kinds of situations, working with and communicating with difficult people, negotiating, selling ideas and methods to co-workers, producing at a high level, working safe, and basically stepping away from the herd and the mediocrity.

Think of the song, "Are You Experienced?" by Jimi Hendrix.

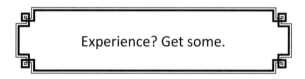
Experience? Get some.

What can you add to your resumé that people don't understand about you?

CONFIDENCE

What comes first, competence or confidence? We could debate this for a while but I think we can agree that one can accompany the other, but not always.

Those who appear most confident usually have put the most practice, planning and preparation into their work, followed by their performance. The 4 Ps feed into everything from careers, sports, the military, business, a good vacation, a healthy family life, a tasty meal … all of it takes effort.

It takes discipline to be confident in most cases, of course ignorance is bliss and some people are simply confident in spite of being woefully inadequate in what they are doing or attempting to do. (Not you, of course.)

If you are the type of person who only believes when you see it, confidence may be hard to achieve. Why not see it when you believe it? Take the best performers and ask them if they visualize their performance before they actually perform. If they are honest, most will admit that they engage in visualization techniques.

They do this because it works. Just imagine if they thought the contrary, if they foresaw failure, defeat and humiliation?

Visualization in and of itself will not get it done, but coupled with effort, focus, practice, work and the right attitude, it will take you a long way.

Are you confident? At what? Make a list.

Now take that well-earned confidence and apply it to other sectors of your life, and do there what you did to get confident in the list you just made.

Get outside of yourself, read, study, ask for a mentor and then listen to that mentor, do for you what a coach would do. Get coachable based on your desire to earn confidence in part based on competence and your life will become different.

You have to fight gravity, every moment of your life.

Think of the song, "Gravity" by John Mayer.

EARNING MONEY VERSUS MAKING MONEY: PEOPLE VOTE WITH THEIR DOLLARS.

You hear people talking all the time about making money, how much they make, want to make, dream of making, yada yada yada.

You do yourself a disservice by thinking in terms of making money versus earning money. It might sound like a trivial difference, but in truth they are as far apart as two words can be. If you work in a mint, you make money, literally.

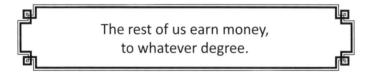

The rest of us earn money, to whatever degree.

When you learn early on in life that in order to earn a certain amount of money you have to perform well at whatever tasks you are given, you learn one of the most powerful lessons.

Just look at those around you, and notice who earns more money and why. Minimum-wage workers earn money commensurate with what they do. Mechanics and technical workers who have learned a trade or gone to school longer earn more. Doctors and what they term as professionals earn even more based on investing their time and what money-learning skills they pick up along the way.

At work, you will see the difference in those who ascribe to the notion of earning their wages versus making money. Those who understand the meaning of these words will arrive early, finish their work on time, inject quality into their tasks, stay late if requested, and generally be an asset to their company. Those who simply make money show up when they do, perform some tasks, place high value on having fun, and then leave when the clock strikes quitting time.

People/companies vote with their money; and money is a limited resource that has all kinds of competing interests vying for it. If you want more dollars, you have to demonstrate value in order to earn the money that those paying / voting are willing to send your way.

> Life is quid pro quo in action, every day, all day, something for something.
> You will have to change / add to / emphasize some aspect of yourself in order to earn the higher amount you seek.

It is fair to say that in a free market economy you get what you earn. If you want to earn more, do more. The market values extraordinary effort and votes with its money to keep or obtain the source of that effort. In this case, that would be you.

When should you start working on yourself and your abilities in order to earn more money? How about nownownownownownownow**NOW**now nownow? (You could wait for one of the next "nows," but … why wait?)

Think of the song, "Money" by Pink Floyd.

Earning versus making, which do you ascribe to?

SELLING? NOT WHAT YOU DO?

What, you a salesperson? NEVER, you say! You would not do that for all the tea in China! Really?

Well, let's face up to the truth. You are selling, all of the time.

Think about it, from the time you could talk and walk, you started by selling your parents on the idea that you were worthy of a new toy, or bike, or costume, or special food for your birthday party and you could list all of the reasons why they should comply with your wishes.

Later on, you were able to sell the local store or business owner to hire you part time, based on your strengths, honesty and work ethic. Not long after this, you had success selling that special someone on the opportunity to go out with you and you then sold them on staying with you and becoming their boyfriend or girlfriend.

As you reached adulthood, you sold your way into jobs, business opportunities, onto sports teams, associations and the like by showcasing your ability to deliver positive results with and for them. Now you sell even more because you have employees to contend with. Perhaps you are married and have to sell your partner on vacation ideas or purchases you want to make. Then comes the children and life has swung full circle as you deal with those eager faces looking up at you and in their best abilities attempt to manipulate you into something you really are not that interested in, but … they will win.

Think of the verbal language you use, the examples of which you make use, and your body language as you conversed with others. You may be a net consumer of other people's ideas or suggestions, but probably you have sold others your fair share of events, or parties, or purchases … but just refused to see yourself as a salesperson.

Think of the language of selling: Hey Billy, let's do this because … the advantage to you is … the real benefit to you is … for example … in your opinion do you feel this is a good idea? You state a claim, back it up with fact, lay out an advantage, followed up with a benefit to them, show evidence and then check back to ensure they are on the same page and … they are yours.

Whether you negotiate on a car, or with a vendor in a stall when on vacation, or with your friends on why they should join you in some activity, you are selling.

In business, people vote with their dollars. If you are in sales, and they are not where they should be, then you have to take a hard look at your package and how it is communicated.

- How is your product knowledge, do you know what you are expected to know?

- What are your mannerisms like? Are you a gentleman businessman?

- Are you punctual for your appointments? Once there, do you deliver a viable proposition?

- How good are your listening skills? Do you seek to understand before you attempt to apply your solution?

- Do you work hard and do other people notice this?

- Do you put others at ease? Are other people comfortable in your presence?

You might not earn your money in direct sales, but it plays a huge role in your life.

How does it feel, you salesperson?

What can you do to improve your ability to communicate and convince?

Think of the book, To Sell Is Human *by Daniel H. Pink.*

MOMENTUM, PROLONGED SUCCESS

Have you ever watched a child push a tire along a road? For a brief time it appears that the tire can continue rolling on its own. In order to maintain the tires trajectory the child is required to provide an occasional shove on the tire or it simply falls over.

Pushing a tire on a flat road or down-hill is easy and can be fun, but … pushing up a steep hill, well that is an entirely different matter. Such is life.

The same goes for everything, every relationship, career, job, … the guy with the nice build who lifts weights three nights a week, the girl with the great hair who wakes up early in order to look the way she does, the man with the great yard who invests four hours a week trimming, cutting, fertilizing, … all of them help the illusion of things continuing on their own.

The point is this, there is no such thing as true momentum. Things do not continue on in perpetuity, everything requires effort or energy of some sort to keep it moving. (Sounds like work!)

There are some who whine and moan about how hard it is to succeed, and the effort required to compete and win. They will carry on about how hard life is and why can't they just have the big house, or large salary, or that nice car, or … a whole host of desirable objects and outcomes.

If these same people invested the amount of time and energy they spend whining, on the work required, they would be a lot closer to achieving those things they dream of having. Work turns dreams into reality.

A dream remains just that, until you put details in place, commonly called a plan, and include work in that plan accompanied with a schedule of the steps and time lines it will take to turn your dream into reality.

Everything and I mean everything takes effort. So if you choose to learn a new skill, or start a work-out program, or begin to learn guitar or piano, get ready to be consistent in your efforts, apply yourself and enjoy the results over the long term, your success at these endeavors depends on you.

Momentum, as fleeting as it is, is enjoyed by those who put the most effort and energy into their life and activities, consistently.

Momentum, build some.

Think of the song, "Like a Rock" by Bob Seger.

COMPETITION

Life is competitive.

We compete for everything from the limited resources that our parents have at their disposal when we are young, to placement at school whether it be in the play-ground or on sports teams or even in the class hierarchy.

Competition is what it is and should be accepted as an integral part of our lives, honing our abilities and forcing us to dig deeper and do the best we can with what we have.

Although it can be hurtful to lose at a game, be over looked for a promotion, be rejected by someone we are competing for, it is the way life is and there is no way around it.

There are some who have succeeded in changing games at school where there are no winners and losers, the kids play a game with no outcome and they all get a trophy. Wow, how does that work? What does the child learn? How can they get better if better is not a part of the game?

Even in societies where everyone is supposed to be equal, some are simply a lot more equal than others. The people who try to sell this kind of political and social framework are also the ones who stand to gain the most. (These people believe in control.)

To live a complete life filled with drama and earned accolades we need to embrace competition, and it starts with competitive games when we are young. The fun is in playing, regardless of the outcome, although winning is much more favorable to losing.

> Life is a marathon and not a sprint, in both cases you still have to run.

Yes there are those who will rise quickly through the ranks — sort of like the rabbit, but the turtle keeps on keeping on, and finishes the race, often winning.

The key here is to be in the race or sport called life. Play the game instead of trying to game the play. Yes there is competition for everything. Get over it.

When the going gets tough, the tough get going. Toughen up! Unless you feel entitled to be at the top of the heap, standing on those who have put in legitimate effort, negating the middle part of your journey where the work and effort reside.

Don't let the numbers get you down. A professional baseball player earning millions tries in vain to bat a thousand, but ends up hitting less than a third of that and goes to the hall of fame as a result. Do the best you can with what you have, and although it is important to know if you are winning, the results will be there when you apply yourself.

Competition? Bring it on.

Think of the book/autobiography,
DRAMA, An Actors Education *written by John Lithgow.*

DISTRACTIONS

Distractions will derail the best and most productive people with good work ethic, what do they do to you?

You see, we are all very capable of being productive and working hard, yes I did say everybody, including you, but you allow yourself to be distracted, or even look for distractions instead of doing the work at hand, and getting it done so that you can move onto the next task, and the next.

An age-old method of getting things done is to complete the hardest and least savoury task first, then everything else gets easier as you work down the list. If you have to eat frogs, eat the big one first.

It is a part of life that you must learn to control, and develop your ability to work with yourself by connecting your mind and body such that they work in unison. After all, the body is capable of anything, almost, but it is the mind that plays games and drifts off to new horizons if left unattended. Engage your mind and, direct your body, remain in the moment.

Thinking is a big part of life as you know, and in particular in dealing with distractions, which after-all are either invited into your life, or they are not. If you are thinking about something, focused, aware of the time and how long the task should take, and working out the details it is harder to be distracted due to your intensity.

If you are haphazardly applying yourself with no definition of the time or result, a lot of things can enter your mind and take you away from what you were doing. The issue with this is that it soon becomes a habit that gets ever harder to break.

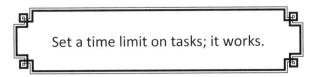

Set a time limit on tasks; it works.

Everything in life is a habit, we habitually through a lack of discipline allow or invite conflicting activities or entities to enter the moment, and we do this moment after moment.

Look at some examples:

- The labourer who has to dig a four-foot hole in the ground on a hot and humid day, he picks up his shovel and takes a few lunges into the rock infested, clay baked, dry as a bone dirt, and then reaches for his phone in order to see if someone has left him a message that will liberate him from the task at hand. He could have the hole dug in about thirty minutes, but he will probably take hours and hours and lose a lot of respect in his boss's eyes, and as he looks in the mirror at break he will also appear smaller as a result of dragging his feet instead of working as he is capable of.

- The office worker who keeps going on line to read about the news, to check out her status and who "likes" her, goes to a chat room, and all of this while being paid, and all of it being observed with the worst of it being they themselves know what they are doing, resulting in their opinion of themselves dropping a notch. (Hard to lie to oneself, isn't it?)

- The salesperson who stops by a coffee shop, too often, stays too long, and has no plan as to how he will earn the money needed to support himself and possibly his family. He has the ability, the market is there for the product or service he represents, and all it takes is to ask questions and then blend the needs of his prospects with the benefits his product delivers and a sale is made. But at the end of the day, with shoulders drooping he will look in the mirror and see a man who is less than he could be, and that image seen day after day will eventually erode his confidence in himself, and he begins to shrink.

You see, what lies right in front of you is up to you to do something with, or ignore, or date and time stamp it for another time. If you deal with what is there now, it is dealt with and you can move on, but by habit if you continue to simply let things pile up, it will get increasingly harder to get to the bottom of the pile and you will suffer as a result.

The person with a messy desk, room, garage, work space, yard ... suffers because if they are honest with themselves and others, they will acknowledge that they want to be neater, that they abhor the mess, but that they are too busy, or there is too much to do, or they will clean it up next week, or ... and of course it never happens.

Do not let distractions derail your vision, effort and work. Choose to learn how to work in a productive fashion and to enjoy the pride of completing a task in a timely fashion and with a good result. Build your legacy one task at a time.

Think of the song, "One of These Days" by Neil Young.

The choice is yours — choose.

And your choice is …………..?

COMPROMISE

When you take a position regarding something you want, or a place you intend to go, a level of earnings you want to achieve, or a type of residence you want to live in, do you get what you want?

How strong is your determination and your power of will, does it embolden you and help you overcome the obstacles that exist between you and almost anything you want?

Negotiating is a part of life, it requires a keen sense of your values, goals or objectives as it relates to you, an understanding of what it will take to achieve those goals or objectives, and if you must deviate from your intended direction, a line in the sand must be drawn regarding what you are willing to compromise on in order to accept less than what you set out for.

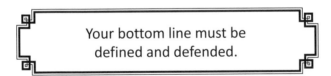

Your bottom line must be defined and defended.

Simply giving in to adversity, or the whim of someone who wants to de-rail your aspirations, or a significant other who argues against what you want, is not developing a compromise, it is just giving up on you, and what you want.

Compromise requires negotiation, discussion, debate, holding your own in the face of a verbal assault and standing tall as you delineate what your absolute minimum requirement is. Some would call this conflict, but in reality it is life and you must become good at protecting yourself from those who would tread over you, while achieving what they want.

If being popular and liked means that you become a door mat by simply laying down as others get their way, is it worth it? Where are you in this scenario? What about your needs and wants?

The next time you are faced with a situation where you know you will run up against someone with a strong will, and especially if they are used to having their way with you, prepare your side of the negotiation, invite them to sit down and then lay out your position and what your minimum requirement is. You will be surprised at the response coming back at you, and it will not be nearly as tough as you imagined.

If in the case of you wanting to earn more money, or having a better job because you know you are worth more and that you can do more, why would you compromise? Is it because there is something called work between you and your desired job or earnings potential? Really?

You would let the requirement for some additional work and effort stop you in your tracks and hold you in the grasp of inactivity? Really?

When you were on the floor, crawling about, drooling, smiling like a fool, and looking up to those bigger than you, at some point you made a choice, stood up which took some effort, then after falling a lot like a drunk person, you learned to walk.

Think of all the lessons you have learned thus far in your life, how did you do it?

You are now walking about this earth just like those big people you used to look up to, you are equal to them, but for some reason you have stopped trying, and are holding onto your current situation. What is it that stopped your momentum, how can it be that you learned so much in a short time early on in your life, and now you are in neutral, glaring into the mirror each and every day?

Compromise if you must, but to simply and repeatedly abandon your wants and needs every time you run up against this thing called work — or someone else's agenda — is not conducive to developing and living a life that you want and can have.

The world is looking for those who will do more, work more, stretch more, suffer through hardship, and lead others through their example. The world will also remunerate those who go the extra mile, stand tall in the face of adversity, and simply "git er dun."

Are you fired up now? Good! Keep blowing on that flame, make it hot enough to melt those obstacles real or imagined and enjoy what is your life, without compromise.

Think of the song, "Where Have I Been All My Life"
by George Strait.

Have you sat down lately and made a list of goals? When will you do so?

III: WHAT'S HOLDING YOU BACK?

CHECKING IN

How has your journey through this book been so far? Have you enjoyed the words and found meaning in the way I applied them, perhaps thinking differently about a few things as a result? How will you use your words? To what end? They are there for you to use and apply.

Will you employ more positive, action-oriented, forward-thinking words as you wind your way further into the trail of your life, building your destiny as you go along?

Will you prefer to use more words of an urgent type? Will you add stronger punctuation? Or, when you are speaking, will you apply stiffer voice intonation to illustrate the need for action and a closing-out of certain events?

Have you discovered new strengths within you? Perhaps ones that can be strengthened even more?

Have you identified any misguided inclinations and bad habits that you want to correct as you move forward in your ever-changing life?

Any new plans in the making, complete with details? Go ahead and list them here:

- Smart goals

- Projects

- New ideas as to what you will do today and in the days that follow

- The people you would like to know as well as the ones you wish to avoid

- Knowledge you want to gain based on experiences or education

- Places where you plan to travel, by a specific time and date

- Health objectives that have been previously overlooked or ignored

- Investment strategies in both finances and time aimed toward a better lifestyle or future retirement

The book, however, doesn't end here. There will be other thoughts that come to mind amid the noise and clutter that have distracted you in the past and are more specific to what you should be doing in the future.

Remain open to these ideas. Do not fall victim to thoughts from your distant past and distorted perceptions of what the future will hold. There is no correlation between the two — unless you consciously want that link to exist. Even so, it is practically impossible to remain in the same situation with the same people for very long. What happened in the past is behind you.

Everything is in flux. What will you do with you while you still have your life and the time that goes with it, hand in hand.

Think of the Stealers Wheel song, "Stuck in the Middle With You."

LIFE IS HARD

These are the opening three words in Dr. M. Scott Peck's book, *The Road Less Traveled*: "Life is hard." He goes on to write that once you accept the fact that life is hard, it no longer becomes hard because you accept it as fact, and follows with a discussion of thoughts and activities that can improve your lot in life.

The term "lot in life" is a variable one. As each moment unfolds, you have the power to choose to act or be acted upon, allow your mind to take in whatever thoughts cross its path, or let it wander aimlessly to wherever you wind up at the end of the day.

Your own lot in life will change by the minute, especially if you are mindfully aware of what is happening around you in real time.

You know that life is hard because of the amount of sweat and toil it takes to earn some of the rewards you get to experience. Sure, it may be easier to load up that credit card on an impulse purchase, but such instant gratification will quickly fade once the bills come in to pay for what might wind up as just another object tossed away in a corner.

Reflection, restraint, discipline, and a chosen direction help ease the burden of life by helping you see all of your options based on your current situation and potential destination.

> Life is hard. But the choices you make will make it harder or less hard.
> Which do you choose?

Hollywood movie stars, rich industrialists, or wealthy Internet wizards all have reaped big financial rewards for their work. Yet we often see or hear reports that expose the dark sides of their lives — drug addictions, alcohol abuse, and other nasty habits. Even with all the money in the world seemingly at their disposal, these people still suffer hardships — self-imposed or otherwise. I used to think it must be easier for them, but, as I have discovered, money in and of itself doesn't make life easier.

So what does lead to a feeling of success that allows you to have love, meaning and close friendships? Simply put, a balance in life.

If you find yourself in the throes of despair, know that suicide is not the answer. Neither is self-flagellation, nor the ingestion of every kind of mind-numbing substance or material to mask the pain, or alter your state of mind.

There is a better alternative.

What you must establish is ownership of this thing called "your life" and to do the best you can with what you have. Face each day with determination, have a clear intent, and follow a list of goals or goals that you will bring closer through your chosen words and actions.

Granted, you might not be embracing the ideal life right now. But what does incessant complaining and moaning accomplish? If anything, staying mired in "woe is me" will drive away those who care about you the most.

Do yourself a favor: Heed whatever solid advice you hear from family and caring friends. Do the work. Expect more and back up your expectations with effort and moxie as you travel the path to success — as defined by you.

Think of the M. Scott Peck book, The Road Less Traveled.

BULLYING

In this day and age, bullying people of any age, sex, religion or race is wrong, unacceptable and should never be tolerated. The word itself simply evokes evil.

Bullying takes two components: the victim and the bully. Remove the victim from that equation, and the bully is neutered, left to his or her own sick and demented tendencies.

Trouble is, though, the bully doesn't want to go away. Instead, he or she will simply move on to taunt the next person in sight. Usually that victim will be smarter, certainly smaller in size, and likely an outcast or loner who will do anything to fit in as part of the bully's entourage.

The bully exists because he or she is taller, larger and meaner, perhaps not as good-looking, and possesses a dark-minded mentality. Such a person does nothing but keep people behind them as a tactic to back up one's so-called leadership. What bullies perceive as "smart" has nothing to do with being educated; instead, it revolves around power: the power to taunt, the power to control and the power to direct people as they see fit.

For the person being bullied, this takes on an entirely ugly reality. The victim is generally timid when near, or in view of, the bully, and fears his or her approach. As the bully builds up a team of followers to support their leader's negative impact, the situation just gets worse.

The bully's incessant verbal and physical attacks are purposely damaging to the powerless victim. It instills fear, groveling, anxiety, depression, pleading, pain, despair and often results in a stunted developmental growth. Victims are left full of self-doubt, instability and with a dimmer view of life as governed by the bully's beliefs. That person may never regain any great level of confidence they might have had beforehand.

Who in their right mind wants to associate with, be friends with, work with or hang around an idiot who bullies people?

It is up to all of us to confront the bullies, and express our clear abhorrence of their tactics, words, actions, and the very nature of their intent. No child, adult, married couple or single person of any background deserves to be bullied.

In some cultures other forms of bullying prevail. Politicians are crooked, and their business associates run the roost as they see fit, squeezing every penny of profit from their poor citizens. Corporations impose their will on the populace to gain even greater profits in spite of the collateral damage they cause. Religion is also used to coerce and control individuals and societies to the detriment of those who participate. As well, gender can be a determinant on freedom. For example, men and women who boldly seek ways to educate themselves, or show any form of self-determination where they break from what is deemed as acceptable behavior, can be reined in, labeled as deviants, and, in many cases, harshly punished by those who seek to control the populace.

Bullying, no matter what form it takes, is a real threat to those who are prone to be victims because of their circumstances, looks, size, race, and gender.

Self-bullying is just as sick. You need to be careful as to what language you use when speaking to yourself. Just because you make a mistake does not make you stupid. Using the wrong word or forgetting something does not reduce your worth nor should it affect your self-esteem.

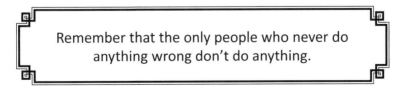

Remember that the only people who never do anything wrong don't do anything.

When you screw up, you're far better off to smile, acknowledge your boo-boo, learn from your error and move on.

If you would stand up to a bully in order to defend others, would you stand up to yourself in order to end the negative self-talk and abuse you accept?

Think of the Don Henley song, "Dirty Laundry."

> Bullying, whether outside of you or inside of you, should never be a part of your life.

Can you think of someone you should confront about his or her bullying?

Think of the Gordon Lightfoot song,
"Sit Down Young Stranger."

FORGIVE AND FORGET

Do you hold a grudge against your cellphone, other electronic device, car, lawnmower, or motorcycle when it breaks down?

Do you blame the meteorologist for the sudden change in weather conditions when they said it would be otherwise?

Are you quick to cuss at every person in the traffic jam (including those damned passengers) that caused you to be late for a meeting, even though you started out intending to be on time?

"Forgive those who trespass against me and I will do the same," or some variation of these words, are not foreign to us. We all like to be forgiven when we make a boo-boo. But wait: that son of a gun did this or said that, or intoned something, or worse yet he or she might have given you "the look" for which there can be no forgiveness.

Ever? Really?

Every day is a new day, and each of these newly minted days comes with a fresh sheet of paper on which you either cut and paste all of the previous days' nasty transgressions, or start afresh.

What will you do?

The people who may have offended you could feel equally as insulted if you ignore them, look away, exclude them in a conversation, give them "the look" and basically help lessen their lives.

Do yourself a favor. Empty your book of transgressions, trespasses and missteps that, in your opinion, others have committed. Encourage yourself to extend a hand to them, to include them, and, though you might never be pals with them, act civil and polite. By doing so, there will be two winners. To a larger extent, you will be the hands-down champion based on how you have grown and are now better equipped to deal with all kinds of people, giving all your perceived offenders another chance.

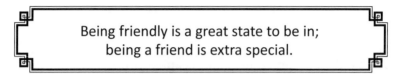

Being friendly is a great state to be in; being a friend is extra special.

The person you most need to forgive, and be friends with, is you. Don't be so hard on yourself. After all, you are learning as you go, aren't you?

Go easy on that person called you.

Think of the Pink Floyd song, "Lost For Words."

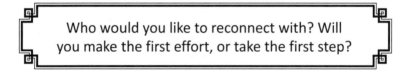

Who would you like to reconnect with? Will you make the first effort, or take the first step?

LIFE IS NOT FAIR

Fair is not something that applies to your life as well as mine. Life is what it is — and from it we build our story. What would a life that is "fair" look like?

Who would decide if something was fair or unfair? What criteria would apply to such a decision? Would anyone agree or disagree with this determination?

In order for you to win, or determine that something was fair, someone else has to lose, or be given the shorter end of the stick, so to speak.

If life were indeed fair, who would clear the forests? Remove all of the stumps? Plant the crops and harvest them? Who would haul the food to market and then spend all day on their feet selling it?

Once the food arrived to your home, who would be the person chosen to clean, cook, serve and then tidy up afterwards?

How would anyone decide who should be a police officer or politician or doctor?

For all of the fair choices made, others will likely fall short of consideration. After all, we can't all be doctors. Who would be the patient?

Fair? Hooey!

If you think in terms of fairness, it might mean you are not thinking of something that you can or should do, and are looking for an easy way out.

The best way to have fairness in your life is to work hard, be honest, apply yourself, and develop multiple options that will address your needs.

The closest to fairness you can get is when you apply effort over an extended time period and, in the process, see that your results are worthy, and that life has been fair to you. This may require you to shift gears, set a new course, work hard, and learn new ways and methods of working.

One lost opportunity does not mean that a person, team or company has been treated unfairly or that the end results are unfair. If after 100 attempts you get zero results, one might think that fairness was not applied. Perhaps that person, team or company is simply not suited for that particular pursuit and would achieve better results in working on a different goal or quest.

You see, fair is a very subjective thing. Each person who views the facts will end up with the scales of fairness being tilted to one side or the other, much like the scales of justice.

Fair, you inquire? Based on whose scales?

Think of the Simon and Garfunkel song, "The Boxer."

CONSEQUENCES

Life without consequences — what would that be like? Would you want it?

If there is one lesson that keeps repeating itself, it's Newton's Third Law of Physics: For every action, there is an equal and opposite reaction.

In your life, this law can be shortened to mean consequences. Sometimes these are hidden; other times, these appear right in your face, and too often ignored. Why?

There are many examples of consequences. Sometimes the end result of an action can produce something positive. In other instances, an improper action may lead to something less desirable. The reaction to either of these may be a delayed one, and hit you when you thought you were in the clear. Ka-Pow!

Let's start by making a short list of the things you can do that have positive consequences:

- Be clear with those who work with, and for you regarding their job and your expectations, train them and ensure they understand the consequences they will experience when they do not perform. This will lead to respect and the results that you are expected to produce with your team.

- Exercise and eating well will lead to good health, looking fit and an earned level of confidence.

- Working hard on the job or at school will lead to promotions, raises, scholarships, and confidence.

- Listening to people and understanding what they mean will lead to friendly exchanges, friends, more opportunities at work and in social circles, plus greater confidence.

- Being honest and straightforward will lead to opportunities at work, with potential mates, and of course, greater confidence from deciding to tell the truth.

Now let's make a short list of those things you can do that have negative consequences:

- Being vague and trying too hard to be liked by those who work with, and for you, leaving others to slack off will result in poor department performance and putting your job at risk.

- Not exercising and eating a diet of fat, sugar and chemical ingredients such as color and artificial flavors will result in poor health, looking unhealthy, being overweight and having low self-confidence and self-esteem.

- Slacking off on the job or at school will result in being fired, demotions, lost opportunities, failure and no higher education resulting in minimum-wage jobs, and little to no self-confidence.

- Talking over people and only about your agenda will result in a narrow circle of people that want to know you and limited to no opportunities at work or socially, and, of course, little to no self-confidence.

- Being dishonest (a liar) and not being straight with people will result in no opportunities at work, very low potential opportunities with any desirable significant other, and a continued draining of any remaining self-confidence.

You see how there are direct consequences that can be measured in dollars and people linked to you, and indirect consequences that are even more valuable but also extremely fragile — lowered confidence levels being most prominent.

Self-confidence comes to you through the application of effort, work, well-thought and executed plans, a knowledge that you can "git 'er dun" and that feeling that you are worth more than what instant gratification can provide you.

There are two ends of every stick you pick up, and on the opposite end can be some nasty stuff.

It is immature and shows a lack of concern for you and others when you haphazardly leap into things without considering the consequences. Slowing down and taking the time from a present-moment awareness (in the gap) is highly recommended and a trait or habit you might want to cultivate in your life.

Think of the George Strait song, "I Can Still Make Cheyenne."

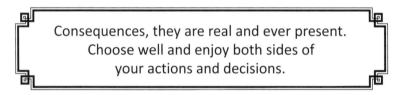

Consequences, they are real and ever present. Choose well and enjoy both sides of your actions and decisions.

Q. Think back to what lessons you have learned from taking actions that were poorly thought out?

"To wear the crown of peace, you must wear the crown of thorns"

These lyrics are from a Gordon Lightfoot song and have always remained with me. Why?

The crown of thorns represents the issues, problems, situations, habits, and thoughts that you encourage in your life through inaction, or by simply not thinking things through and winding up in situations you could have avoided. (Again!)

It is true that you can learn from your mistakes. But how many times do you need to do the same mistake before you "get it?"

The person who wears the crown of peace represents a considered life, one in which reflection and thought was expended in order to limit the missteps one might have taken. It is about accepting where one is at the moment while working towards those things that they value and want in their lives. Friends, associates, allies, and others who are willing to help are recruited to provide an individual with advice and experiences as he or she works towards defined goals.

There is peace in having a plan, working on that plan and enjoying the results.

There are always thorny issues, but you can occasionally get by them with minor scratches. The best plan is to stay completely away from the thorns — just don't go there.

I would suggest that you don't gather enough thorns in your life to build a crown.

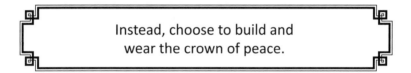
Instead, choose to build and wear the crown of peace.

Think once more of the Gordon Lightfoot song,
"Sit Down Young Stranger."

WISH YOU WERE BETTER RATHER THAN THINGS BEING EASIER

How many people do you know who wish they were better, more adept, had more knowledge, and were capable of doing more in certain areas of their life, job, sport, or the economy — and then did something about it?

Doing something might include taking night courses, networking with groups in your desired field of interest, studying online or buying books that cater to improving a subject of interest and learning the basics upon which you can build.

Getting better at something takes effort. It might also require shedding old and useless habits that do little except keep you stuck in the same place, repeatedly doing the same thing, with the same people and coming up with the same results and excuses. (Among other names, this has often been called insanity!)

Being better at something is important, as long as you base it on your personal standards. Don't start comparing yourself with the elite in a particular field of endeavor. Just be honest with yourself and take the necessary steps, one step at a time and work your way up to greater competence, agility, ability and knowledge.

Improving your skills and abilities will ultimately get you to where you want to go, and lead to the achievement of those goals you have outlined and have been currently tracking.

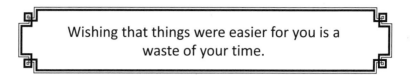

If things were made easy for you, for how long would you enjoy them? What do you do with those things that are free and given to you without making any effort?

Take time as an example. It is given to you, but ... what do you do with it? Really?

It is your choice, at every moment of every day, to do something or nothing. You can pick a direction and get moving. Or do nothing and stay put.

Your move. What is the choice you have just made? When will you support that choice with action? Now would be a good time.

Think of Helen Keller,
and read her autobiography for some inspiration.

"A BIRD SEARCHING FOR A CAGE" (BLOG BY SETH GODIN)

How creative are you? Can you extricate yourself from situations or problems into which you have put yourself? Do you find yourself trapped, as though you were in a cage?

How did you get there? Was the door wide open and you just flew in? Why? Because it was easy?

The aforementioned cage can be simple: services to which we hastily agree but lock us in, creating undue stress living up to very high expectations. The cage can also reflect a relationship with someone who we really like but also include troubling aspects such as them being very sloppy, demanding, bullying, a liar and/or a substance abuser. As well, the cage might be in the details of the job description you accepted — terms that you find out later are caustic and ruinous to your wellbeing.

You may have constructed the walls of your cage in order to avoid what you should be doing, or as a way of self-imprisonment.

You, imprisoned? Well, if you feel as though you are caged in and held back due to circumstances and limitations that, with effort, you could possibly erase, then that is a form of incarceration, one of your making and that you could unmake by your own admission.

Just look at all of the dilemmas you have dealt with thus far. Examine how you made the decisions that led you out of that cage and then look at the next steps you took that put you into the next or current dilemma/cage. (Life is full of them.)

Is a life with someone choking you with their noxious demeanor reason enough to continue with them? If you are in a job that you simply abhor, and that you work at only because of the money, is the money worth it? With the job market constantly changing, if you were to apply some effort and take a night course in college, would that free you from the cage and let you fly to a new perch?

Of course, perspective matters in these cases. Are you looking at the situation or person or job in the proper light? Have you done all you can do in a spirit of co-operation to make the situation better? Have you given up too soon and not learned a lesson as a result?

Is the cage you are in based on your limited ability, or unwillingness to communicate in a clear and adult fashion? Do those who peer into your cage understand the true nature of why you are there?

The cage is obviously used here as a metaphor. Still, it can be just as confining and limiting as the steel structure of a prison, and, in many cases, can restrain you for your entire life.

It is incumbent upon you to reflect on your life, your relationships, job, finances, health and other matters on a regular basis to ensure you don't build a cage or step into one.

Being set free in a free-market economy does have some responsibilities attached to it. Work is there for you to do. For some people, though, this is a hard concept to accept as they believe they just have to do little to nothing and everything will fall in their laps — and that too can be considered a cage.

Think of the Beatles song, "The Long and Winding Road."

Or,

the Jon Kabat-Zinn book Wherever You Go, There You Are: Mindfulness Meditation in Everyday Life.

Do you see that all roads lead to you?

OBSTACLES TO YOU BEING IN THE MOMENT, AS IN HERE AND NOW

Obstacles? What obstacles can there be?

One simple answer: You!

I'm not sure that there is a conspiracy going on, but it sure seems that a lot of enterprises benefit from you and I being in "their" moment. Commercials, Web sites, promises … all aimed at keeping you in their court, luring you in believing what they want you to think.

Food, beverage and snack ads all beckon you to consume. Clothes commercials show off models who are so skinny, they look as though they should be at the doctors, or at least at the nutritionists, before their clothes fall off.

Headphone manufacturers beg you to listen to their sound systems, both big and small, so that you can fill your life with more noise — lest you drift into the moment and see all of these distractions for what they are.

Alcohol purveyors offer their many colours, tastes, container configurations, and emphasize which group or cult personally suits you best by simply consuming their particular brand of booze. Really? (it is just alcohol, in many guises.)

Lawyers will have you know that if you make a mistake, slip and fall, have an accident … that not only will you be exonerated, but in the process, they will fetch you a bucket full of money.

Game sellers elicit pure animal/survival instinct based on the premise that it is you against everyone else. By purchasing their products, you can form a team to help you, but it is your ability to kill and maim as many others as you can that will ultimately make you a winner.

Some religions beseech you to join their ranks in order to fulfill their destiny. The more cultish ones may use their words and so-called reasoning to brainwash you to kill, destroy, gather money for them, or build elaborate buildings to attract even more unwitting people into their dark web.

The morning news, tweets, notices, billboards.... ahhhhhhhhhhhhhhhhhhhhhhhhhhhhhhhhhhhhhhhhhhhhhhhhhh (think of a scream)!

Whew! Doesn't that all sound stifling, choking, gagging, and controlling?

What do you think would be the greatest fear from all of these companies and those who profit from you buying or consuming ever greater quantities of their products? That you will find silence, peace, understanding, love, self-respect and the feeling that "you are enough" without them.

Where are you in all of this?

Take a walk, by yourself, without that damned electronic device tracking your every move and keeping you tethered to what you don't need. Let your mind drift and get quiet as you distance yourself from all of the aforementioned noise and influences. Just keep walking and enjoy the peace of being alone.

Breathe deeply. As thoughts or images enter your mind, ignore them and remain with a light awareness of the breaths you inhale and exhale. Once you reach a calm state of mind, pose questions to yourself and let the answer come to you. Listen to the wisdom that resides within you.

You need to hear the answer.

Ultimately, the biggest obstacle to you being in the moment is, well, you. Take a stand, and make a choice to be silent and perhaps start meditating. Once you start and stick with it every day, your practice will improve with time and effort.

There are no free rides.

Think of the song, "Silence," by Richard Morin (me).

MEDITATION

When you are born, you are naked in many ways. Just look at any baby and watch how he/she interacts with the world. As long as babies are warm, fed, dry, cuddled or given your attention, they are content.

From their perspective, babies see the world in wide-eyed wonder and accept things for what they are. They don't hate a certain color, day of the week, type of person, different foods, political parties … they just look, accept and move on.

When you wake up in the morning, you are also naked in many ways.

However, as you prepare to face the day, you also wrap your mind up with thoughts, doubts, the previous day's issues, fears of tomorrow, and so on.

A lot of what you take on in the morning is a repeat from so many other mornings, carryovers from another time and place, some issues being habitual and deeply ingrained.

Habits can be good when it is good for you, such as a daily exercise routine, maintaining a good diet of nutritious food, working hard and staying focused.

Automatically loading up with the same old thoughts and fears is not one of those good habits.

When you take time to sit and meditate, preferably in the morning soon after you get up, you can become more aware of how quickly negative thoughts can absorb you — much like the way a mummy is wrapped, leading to an unrecognizable person.

Stop wrapping yourself with all of these layers. Remain like the furrows of a freshly tilled garden and allow the sun from each new day to provide energy to new thoughts and adventures based on acceptance. Dispose of those words and thoughts that conspire to cloud over the day you're trying to savor.

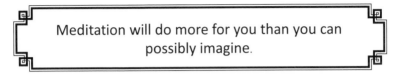

Meditation will do more for you than you can possibly imagine.

You will become aware of life around you and the sounds and smells that accompany each moment. You will learn that your breath becomes the magic carpet on which you float — not concentrating on it, but simply being aware of it and getting into the ebb and flow of the incoming and outgoing breaths. You'll enjoy the gap between the two and realizing that life in the gap is free from the opinions, judgments and noise of a burdened mind.

It does take effort, but please, right now, write down all of the good things in life that come for free. Short list, isn't it? (Time should be at the top of that very short list.)

I recommend a 15-minute regimen that start with a few yoga moves, and culminates with you sitting in the Lotus position, cross-legged on the floor, eyes closed and simply being aware of your breath. Can you afford 15 minutes in the morning to do this? Really?

As you learn to stay centered, using the rhythm of your breath as your companion, you will soon learn to only take on those things in your mind that you need or want, dispensing the rest of the flotsam and jetsam that too often bury the real you.

You may clearly understand what the word meditation means, or you may just have a vague idea of what meditation is, based on movies you have seen, but ... I urge you to search the true meaning of meditation.

For me? Meditation has meant a deeper appreciation of life, a more Eastern take on my interactions, instead of the current Western consumption-based frenzy I have applied to my days. (I *still* have so far to go, as I find myself caught up in the various frenzies that make up my day.)

You may learn to question certain aspects of your life and how you have been choosing to live it. It may become evident that faster is not better, or that more simply weighs you down. You may discover that non-stop sound and visual stimulation from your electronic gadgets leaves no time for you — time to actually be in the moment to smell all the smells, hear the sounds of others, feel the texture of life and those people and things with which we come into contact. This is just like the move, "Eat, Pray, Love" where Julia Roberts is inside the temple and for 60 seconds you see myriad thoughts rolling through her head like a raging river, which seems a lot longer than 60 seconds.

I used the word "thoughts" in this particular instance, but in truth, the raging current of images, and language that plague your mind are mainly comprised of not actual thoughts, but merely noise. A thought requires a true examination or attempt at learning, seeing, hearing, feeling whatever other people, activities, issues, problems or opportunities enter our conscience as we make our way through our day.

Conscious thoughts have a life because we have created them. These are real thoughts from which we can build, take with us, explain, use, and elaborate.

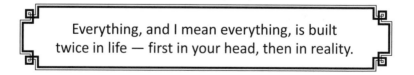

Everything, and I mean everything, is built twice in life — first in your head, then in reality.

The noise in our heads is just that: noise.

When I suggest "think good thoughts," which is how I close out most emails that I send, what I mean is for you to think what you want to think, apply your mind to the tasks and activities that you want to, as opposed to having vast periods of your day and life lost in a cloud of disconnected noise.

Meditation is worth your effort. Please take my word on it and make the effort to connect with life and experience the full range of possibilities and the realities that make up what is your life.

Why not? You have tried everything else, try this, you have everything to gain and nothing to lose.

Will you invest $20 in a book or DVD on the topic? It can only help.

Think of the Jimmy Cliff song, "I Can See Clearly Now."

THINKING GOOD THOUGHTS (WHAT OTHER KINDS ARE THERE?)

That depends on you, and how you are able to maintain your focus and stay on task as you work through your day and life. If you are afflicted with mind-numbing floods of noise, fears, doubts, scenarios constructed by your vivid imagination that drowns out what is a peaceful day or moments in your life, then you know what good thoughts are versus the opposite.

When you think the opposite of habitual thoughts that are not positive, you will have started to create a good habit.

- Think of love, peace, friends, family, opportunities that are within your reach.

- If the news and media fill your mind with negative and hurtful thoughts and images, turn them off.

- Instead of thinking you better hurry or you might be late and catch hell from your bosses as a result, think of getting there early and benefiting from a calmer start to your day.

- Rather than thinking that you should call up so and so because it has been a while and they will be annoyed, think about calling them now or more often in order to inject some energy into their life.

- As opposed to saying to yourself that you better exercise or you will turn into flab, think about getting into your exercise regimen because you want to look as good as you can.

- Instead of keeping a scale in front of the refrigerator as a reminder to not eat certain foods because you are overweight, buy the right foods for yourself and your family because you want to be healthy. Limit the damage done by sugars, white flour, food color, flavors, and other poisonous combinations. Put that scale in the bathroom or walk-in closet.

- Wash your clothes and clean your body not because it smells bad but because you want to smell and look as good as you can.

- Ignore the clock as it gets towards the end of the day and instead of looking over your shoulder, finish the work you started even if it takes you an extra few minutes and enjoy the fact that you are done, and can start afresh the next day, enjoying the recognition this kind of effort brings.

You can buy fiction books that deal with all kinds of tragedy, terror and murderous acts, but leave those types of thoughts between the covers of those books. Instead, cultivate the plans you have for yourself and attend to all of the details that will make those plans come to life, commit to effort and pull together the resources and ingredients it will take to make it all come true.

Choose what you think and enjoy the results. You have a clean slate to work with today. What will you jot down on it and how will it govern your actions on this day?

Thinking good thoughts is a habit. Thinking bad or negative thoughts is also a habit. Smiling comes easy when you think good thoughts; frowning occurs in part when you dwell on the negative and remain in its grasp.

> **Think good thoughts, smile, build it into a habit ... today!**

Think of this book, and how it might be worth reading over certain sections in order to make a commitment, and get into thinking good thoughts and actions, which will lead you to where you really want to be, and can be.

HANGING ON (PERSPECTIVE)

Do you feel as though you are just hanging on to life by a thread or the skin of your teeth, straining to see the value and too often examining the reasons why you should continue?

Perspective helps dissolve these feelings. Perspective provides you a lens that you can use to measure your life, much like a ruler or tape measure allows you to grade the length or height of something.

To better develop your perspective, you need to see how other people live and what they do to get through their lives each day. Considering other people is not the same as comparing, though — and it's important to understand the differences between the two.

There are some people born with very limiting physical or mental impediments, and yet these individuals seem to have a strong sense of joy and attack life in their way. Despite whatever their situations might be, these very same people still go out to find work, have their own place to live, use public transit, and simply do the best they can with what they have, smiling through their day.

There are some countries where the conditions are extremely challenging and limiting, with highly populated cities and limited sources, and yet these people work hard at life, and also do the best they can with what they have.

There are so many examples of differing perspectives. Just look around you. Invest the time in understanding why you think what you think, how that affects what you do, and how thinking differently will give you a new sense of self that will help you see your opportunities.

> Perspective will help you see that your situation is not permanent. There are actions you can take now that will alleviate or impact your situation in a positive way.

Unless you have done everything, learned everything, spoken with every available person or agency, asked for help from every person you know, reached out to all supports groups, and done all the rest of the things that you can do, then you have no reason to allow despair to grip and paralyze you.

Life is hard, there is no way around it. You have to cut through it and do the best you can with what you have. Work with that. Show yourself what you can do in spite of the impediments. Become a mentor to others who will rally around your words and follow your example.

Life gets better. Write down what you will do, today, tomorrow, the days after that … and then do it.

Think of Stephen Hawking, who was told he would live two years, when he was 21.
(He's now 73!)

Or,

in a more stark fashion, the opening of Hannibal Lecter's, "Dear Clarice" speech in the film "Hannibal" starring Anthony Hopkins.

"WHEN YOU ARE GOING THROUGH HELL, KEEP GOING."
WINSTON CHURCHILL

During the Second World War, when the V1 and V2 rockets sent over as a gift from Germany were raining down on London, England, and despair was common and everywhere, the great orator Winston Churchill gave one of his most spirited and emotional addresses to the people of his country.

The gist of his message was simple: "When you are going through hell, keep going!"

He urged his people, the same ones who elected him, who looked up to him, and to whom he owed his livelihood to keep going, to not stop, to contribute and to help each other out and do the best they could with what they had.

Those were hard times by any measure.

You, however, are not living in wartime-era England; bombs and rockets are not falling on your head. But in too many instances you pause and crouch down from incoming issues and problems instead of rising up and dealing with them. Why? Is there a lesson here for you? What is holding you back? What have you to fear but fear itself?

The clues might be outside of you, but the answers come from within. You might ask your friends, family or a counsellor what you should do. But in truth, how can anybody else really know the answer?

If you are not pleased with your current situation, and you know you have a lot more capacity within you, strike out in a new direction. Seek out a course or book on a topic that interests you and then find a place in which you can apply that new knowledge and the passion you have for doing that kind of work.

What are you waiting for? A bomb to fall on your head?

Stand up! Keep moving! As Winston Churchill also once said, "Never, never, never give up."

Think of the B.J. Thomas song,
"Raindrops Keep Falling On My Head."

SILENCE AND REFLECTION

There is so much going on in your life: the need to sleep, cook, eat, wash dishes, shop for food, clean yourself, tidy up your living spaces, commute, work, take care of others, build, maintain and have relationships, and perhaps have time left over for yourself. What can you cut out or perhaps reduce so that you can have time to simply sit in silence and think/reflect on your life, activities, and learn from what you have done so far?

Those who write books have to stop every so many pages, go back, reflect, correct, change, erase, adopt new words and meanings, then tackle it again and again in order for the book to be palatable in the hopes of selling more books than the number that makes up their family.

Now … what about your book/life? Is there any reflecting going on? Really? What new chapters are you creating?

Has social media overgrown its importance? Is it critical to be "liked" by those who do not even really know you? (Think mirror!) What about LinkedIn? Twitter? What of the other noise that so willingly wants to monopolize any spare moment you might have?

With life truly being a mental journey accompanied by your body, making moments in your day for you — and only you — is a very worthwhile investment. How else will you ever realize where you are now, and where you are going?

Turn off all of the noise, reduce your need to validate yourself as often as you do, be proud of who you are, what you are doing, and what you are thinking within your life. This is your life, right?

Not knowing about everything that is going on in the world or with others is OK. These are of no value to you either way. You are not worth less or more if you engage in the transfer or creation of more noise for others to glance at and then move on.

If you were to take a test at the end of a day, week, month, or year about the accuracy of what you have read or heard on the Internet or broadcast news, and whether you passed or failed, would it all matter?

Some things need to be repeated, like this paragraph. Leave your electronic device behind you. Take a walk around your neighborhood. Find a trail in the woods. Go sit by a lake or river, and revel in its beauty and real qualities. Turn off all of the media and sit back in a comfortable chair. Or engage in meditation as a means of getting back to the real you, the human being who is the center of what is your life.

The captain of any ship or aircraft updates his position often throughout the journey. They check fuel, maintenance of the craft, people in key positions, passengers if applicable, and then measure all of that against their intended destination. (They also plan for alternates, in case any bad things happen.)

The captain cannot, and does not, engage in 50 activities at once. He goes through his checklist, considers the information, is connected to "relevant" channels of communication, makes the necessary corrections, and delivers his vessel to the proper destination on time.

So, captain, where are you now? Where are you going? When have you planned to arrive? Are you on course? Really? How do you know?

Think of the Christopher Cross song, "Sailing."

MENTAL AND PHYSICAL JOURNEY: WHAT YOU THINK AND DO IS UP TO YOU.

There are two parts to you, and some would argue that there are three were you to count the spiritual portion.

What happens to you physically almost entirely relies on what you think, and what you direct your body to do. The way some people treat themselves is as though they do not see the connection between body and mind and how these could be in harmony leading to new and different outcomes.

The piper is playing a tune in your life and someone has to pay the piper, and that person is you!

Think of yourself as the puppeteer holding the strings to your puppet (your body), making it jump around and dance as long as you pull the right strings. It can also lie still in a crumpled heap without any direction from you.

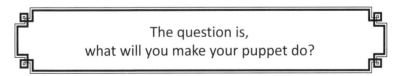

The question is, what will you make your puppet do?

Exercise or stay on your couch. Work hard or slack off. Eat well or poorly. Drink water or liquor. Read or watch TV. Show up on time or late. Smoke cigarettes or quit, Do drugs or stay clean. Study or give in to distractions. Hang around with influential people or the bad crowd.

Any one of these can have an impact on how you and your body looks, feels, performs, and holds up.

You need to be careful, as carelessness or lack of discipline and direction can lead you and your puppet to an addiction. Addictions are a challenging topic, but the best way to beat an addiction is to avoid getting one if you can. Before you say yes, or start something, think about where it leads, pull the right strings in order to escape the peril. This may appear so obvious, and it is. So why do people make such bad choices throughout their lives incurring the damage they do to themselves and others?

Discipline plays a huge role in your life and is probably the single biggest determinant in how you will turn out or how you make it through your life. There is a need within you to think and then apply those thoughts in a way that moves you forward toward what you want and can obtain.

Work is ever present, and you either choose to do the work, put off the work, or hide from it. If you combine discipline with a work ethic, you have a powerful combination that will accomplish amazing feats in your life.

Opportunities are always in front of you (never behind), and by harnessing your mental and physical combination you can choose to take them on. Discipline and a strong work ethic applied through the strings to your puppet (meaning you) will have you dancing the way you want.

Think of the Moody Blues song, "The Best Way To Travel."

Q. How are you at pulling your own strings? Do you work at getting better each day?

The music is playing — care to dance?

SETTLING FOR LESS? WHY?

What do you want out of your life? Have you written it down? With dates? Really?

Now go get it, make it happen. Research what it takes to obtain that thing you just defined. Go after it with all of the zeal you can muster and stay with it.

The river of time eventually runs out. Right now, though, you are flowing down that river, every second of your life, as you navigate its channels and make use of those things that come within your grasp.

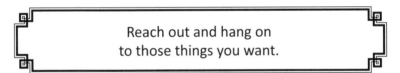

Reach out and hang on to those things you want.

Are your friends burdening you with their fears and concerns for your wellbeing? With their "well-meaning" doubts and concerns for you, are they grating on your fragile psyche, and keeping you in place as a result? Do the words "be careful" come at you too often?

Have those rude and shallow comments from past teachers and coaches lingered in your memory?

Look in the mirror and be honest with yourself. If you have the basic ingredients to achieve what you want, and the only thing holding you back is effort and work, stop making excuses and do it.

Don't ask for permission. From who will you ask?

When you read the biographies of those people who rank high enough in our collective esteem, you learn that they did not ask for anything. They broke rules, established new ways of doing things, fought off those who weighed them down, and they just kept at it when mere mortals would have given up and watched TV.

So … are you settling for less? Do you want to list the reasons why you are doing so? Go ahead do it here in this book or a notebook.

Now … make another list containing the reasons why you deserve more, and what it will take to get what you want, and have more instead of less. Do it now.

I am sure your list of reasons why you should have more will be a lot longer and contain more emotion than the restrictive list of reasons why not.

Go ahead, sharpen your pencil and start now. Write the list, now. Do it, NOW.

Think of the Michael Michalko book,
Thinkertoys: A Handbook of Creative-Thinking Techniques.

YOUR FIREWALL: NO ONE CAN MAKE YOU FEEL INFERIOR WITHOUT YOUR CONSENT.

What is it with praise that has us so desperate to seek it? How can a frown be so heavy and lasting in our mind, while a light, pleasant smile is so fleeting in its effect on us?

If we are all considered equal, how can it sometimes not feel that way?

The truth is, we are all equal as well as unique. We just need to look around to see that this is a fact. The evidence is overwhelming.

If a tall man is six feet and an average man is five feet, ten inches and a short man is five feet, eight inches, how can we let four inches affect us? Why does that even matter? When you walk along a beach and see throngs of people of various shapes and sizes in their swimsuits, it should have the effect of calming your anxieties and helping you see that you're not all that different from many of the people on that beach.

Certainly there are those shapely men and women who are into bodybuilding and fitness. But are the hours a week that they invest in their bodies worth the effort, when we know that the moment they stop they will return to the shape that their job and lifestyle requires?

> Physical fitness is one thing.
> Vanity fitness is something else.

Catalogues are full of young shapely women. But when I walk through a shopping mall, I don't see very many of them. Why is that? What is it with people who are not like us, modeling the clothes that marketing companies want us to wear?

The important thing to remember is that you are you. You should accept you as you are, while applying effort towards enhancing your skills, abilities, language, knowledge and appearance — minus all those feelings of ineptness and unworthiness that you allow to creep into our mind.

You will never know everything that others know, and why should you? Good conversations come from hearing people speak about things of which you have little or no knowledge. If everyone knew everything about the same things, what the heck would you discuss?

So dress up that body of yours. Strike out into the world of people and engage in conversations and activities.

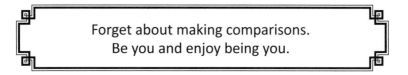

Forget about making comparisons.
Be you and enjoy being you.

Think of this book, and what you have read thus far.
Do you see you more clearly?

SUFFERING

Everyone suffers to some extent. You don't have to be poor, living in a shelter, or wasting away from malnourishment to know what suffering is.

Suffering is a private matter. Most people do not share their pain, issues and especially what is often perceived as mental illnesses.

You see people laughing and having a grand ol' time, surrounded by throngs of people who love them. As you stand by yourself on the fringe, you are probably wondering, "What is the matter with me?"

Well, frankly, there is nothing wrong with you. You are you. The question you might ask is this: What have you been doing to improve your social circumstances? Have you struck up any conversations with strangers lately?

You could ask yourself how many clubs or associations have you joined lately? Have you participated in actual live, in-the-flesh events or gatherings, as opposed to wearing your thumbs out checking out social media?

Another query that could be relevant: Have you let your friends know that you are looking to get busy, that you want to meet people and are willing to go to new lengths (for you, that is) to meet others?

Answer these and the other questions that follow the same train of thought, and you will see that there is nothing wrong with you at all. The issue has been your methods. Change your methods and the results will change.

Although suicides are not publicized, there are an awful lot of them and many could have been avoided if the person would have simply come forward with their problems, listened to suggestions on how to handle them, and then took up the reins in their life.

As you deal with the many challenges life throws at you, remember that your problems are not that unique. What is different is the way you look at them. By changing the way you look at things, you change the very nature of them. The challenge is to look at each situation or challenge in as many different ways as you can.

In his book, *Thinkertoys: A Handbook of Creative-Thinking Techniques* Michael Michalko takes you through many different ways to think, using methods he coaches you to use.

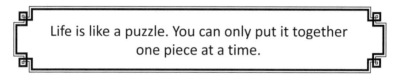
Life is like a puzzle. You can only put it together one piece at a time.

In life, each piece interconnects with many others to form a complete picture. You cannot circumvent the process, in real life or while completing a puzzle. It is a meticulous and time-consuming task that all of us have to figure out. It is OK to ask for help in seeing the maze, or in identifying the piece needed to continue, but you have to put the piece in place.

Suffering is painful, and hard to explain to those who do not seem to have the time or capacity to listen. That said, just as in all things in life, the healing process is up to you, just like physiotherapy follows an operation.

Read, think, reach out to others, and do things differently every day. Suffering continues unabated if nothing changes; hence the need to change and apply new thoughts and actions to your life.

Suffering? Keep reading, thinking and working with yourself. Life gets better.

Once again, think of the Michael Michalko book,
Thinkertoys: A Handbook of Creative-Thinking Techniques.

INTERNAL CONFLICT (ANXIETY)

Do you suffer from internal conflict, also considered to be anxiety? The thoughts, noise, feelings, or voices that conspire to sink your self-esteem, make you doubt yourself, your abilities, your worth, and as a result, shrinking your options by keeping you in place?

Are you subjected to an endless stream of random thoughts that run counter to what you so want to have in your mind, and, by extension, in your life?

Are there times you just want to scream at all those nonsensical, negative, abusive or painful thoughts that rapidly fly in and out of your mind?

The public, your family, and even your closest friends see you as they do, dressed as you are, smiling, and seemingly without much of any stress or issues blocking your path. But the truth is that you may have another side of you, one that, contrary to your public persona, creates havoc. It invokes doubt and worry and generates so many incomprehensible and painful scenarios.

If none of this applies to you, then good for you. Move on to the next chapter as you are blessed. (Ten points for you!)

If some of this does appear in your life, then the question is this: What do you do about it?

An empty agenda is fertile ground for these dissenting and self-loathing voices. When you are busy, engaged in some activity, working, reading, studying, practicing, playing a musical instrument or a sport, truly engaged in your job, with your family and friends, or solving a problem, you are able to remain in the moment much more easily, without being bothered by this internal dialogue.

Engagement is a key element in dealing with this.

The solution is not based on consuming readily available drugs, whether they are of the prescribed type or the illegal sort, or alcohol, or some ritualistic religion that has you spending your valuable time in prayer. (Although some of this might apply in certain situations.)

The real solution is found within you, through discipline and examination, and the building of an agenda that keeps you working, focused and building something you want and value within you, and your life. Looking outside of you for a solution is the easy way out, but what does that solve? If you can't talk over the noise in your head, keep it at bay through activity and better use of your mind, do with your power of thinking as you will. It takes effort, but what else are you to do?

When you find yourself in turmoil, not sure what to do or say, spinning around in your head, you have to look up, identify a task or chore that needs doing and you have to get started. Always start by doing something.

Whether it is taking a shower, washing the car, cooking, returning a phone call, or whatever, just do it. Then once you have completed that task, move on to the next item, and the next, until you regain your balance. Holding your head will do nothing for you. Looking outwards for a drink or some drug might provide some short-term relief, but the core issue needs to be worked on. Activity is a way to engage your mind and empower action that leads to completion of something and the confidence that you can do it as a result.

Another strategy is meditation, to simply sit down, and become aware of your breathing. In the time you are sitting on the floor, legs crossed and simply opening up your awareness to the present moment, you will soon escape the grip anxiety has on you, allowing a reconnection with the activities and thoughts that preceded it.

It is so worth your time to look into meditation.

Reading sometimes helps, as does speaking with someone who knows you and understands the nature of your issue. But most people who suffer from anxiety do so in private, afraid to share their problem in part because it is hard to explain.

How do you explain what anxiety is to someone, when by all appearances you have a lot going for you? It could be that you have a good job, money, a nice house, or perhaps you are a good musician or have lots of friends and enjoy a great social life.

The future is in front of you. We all know this. But too often that very future seems to be buried under all kinds of stuff of which you have no need like worries, fears, frustration, stress and the nagging suspicion that you are not up to the task at hand. Forget all that unnecessary stuff. The sun will rise tomorrow. There will be new people, new customers, new and different jobs or opportunities. All these will be readily available to you provided that you help yourself, network with others, and of course, work.

Let people know you are looking to change jobs, or join a team, or help out some charity. Sharpen some skills that you know are of value in the marketplace. You will have a chance at other relationships, or the option of a different place to live. So you see, being stuck in the past is really not an option. You must keep pace with the day and what comes with each day.

This is something you have to step into. Develop the habit of getting things done, and then move on to the next tasks at hand.

I know life is hard and that appearances are just that. But you have the power to do something, and build on that something every day of your life. If you want change, then change. It all starts with you, ends with you, and will always be up to you. Talking if it leads to action is good.

If talking leads to just more talking and hand-wringing, then you have to make a decision.

Start now. It only gets better. Become a person of action to bury your little secret.

One day at a time.

Think of the song, "Guaranteed"
sung by Eddie Vedder from the movie soundtrack,
"Into The Wild."

ONE DAY AT A TIME

Alcoholic Anonymous have it right: Life, success, love, relationships, sobriety, growth, learning … these are all based on one day at a time.

By focusing on "one day at a time," you get to do your best work, of the highest quality, most productively, and you have more control based on your appreciation of the current day.

One day at a time requires you to leave yesterday behind. You already lived that day; now you need to live this one. Fortunately, you don't have to become an alcoholic to know the truth of the words they repeat all day long: One day at a time.

You don't have to lose friends, jobs, opportunities, and other important aspects to your life just because you do too much of something un-important and not enough of what is important.

You have 86,400 seconds in a day. I know, who wants to be always cognizant as to how much time they have used, or have left. Well … you can live blindly or you can at least keep an eye on the gauge and live accordingly.

With 86,400 seconds a day, and if you live sixty years, you will have 21,900 days, or 18,921,600,000 seconds to live the life of your choosing, based on circumstances of course and importantly what you do within those circumstances.

So if you do the math, and you are twenty, thirty, forty, fifty, sixty, seventy, eighty, or … you get a clear picture of how much is left in your tank.

> Long-term plans and goals are great. But each one only gets closer one day at a time.

Borrowed or purchased time? Nice idea, but … not realistic.

Think of the Alan Jackson song, "Amarillo."

REFLECTION: A CONSIDERED LIFE

An unconsidered life is one that might not be appreciated. It offers little to no definition, perhaps left to be constantly tossed about like windswept tumbleweed crossing the Texas, Utah, and Arizona deserts.

I will share with you a recording I once heard that prompted a great deal of self-reflecting:

> Imagine you are walking down a long, narrow, gravel road, the wind is blowing softly across your face, teasing your hair. What you hear is the wind as it blows past your ears and through the leaves of the small trees that line the ditch. The crops are waving at you from the field, their scent is inviting, and the sun caresses your body as you stroll down this quiet road, in a mood of inquiry and examination.
>
> Off in the distance on a gentle rise, you see a large oak tree with its thick branches making a great canopy, like an umbrella you might say. As you approach the tree you note that there is a person sitting on a stump in the shade and they are watching you as you make your way up the slope.
>
> As you get closer you can see that this person is clearly interested in you and is now leaning forward in a pose of expectation, awaiting your arrival.
>
> You cross the barbed-wire fence, and are now standing in front of this person extending your hand in a greeting, when you realize that this person is you when you were a child, and they recognize you as the person they will become.

What would you say, and what would this other person say to you? What warnings, or advice would you extend to them, and what would this individual offer you as they see the person they will become? Where would the conversation go?

Reflection from time to time is a good thing. However, like all things, too much of it reduces its value and takes you away from the now and your forward attention.

In the case of the story I just recanted, it is possible that a lot of good could come from self-reflection. It would depend on how honest you are with yourself and your willingness to accept, forgive and forget those parts of the past that haunt you.

There is value in knowing and understanding those things that have brought you to the point at which you are now. But, just like the rear-view mirror, all that is required is a glance to what is behind you, lest you crash into what lies in front.

If you want to reflect on your past, do so when you have the time to do it well, perhaps upon completing your daily meditation.

Think of the Supertramp song, "Crime of the Century."

PRIVILEGE

What do you think of the privilege you have been granted in the form of your life right now, in this economy, with your abilities and the opportunities that await you?

This is a loaded question. Some people who read this may be facing some huge obstacles every day of their lives, and yet they are able to occasionally smile through their days while doing the best they can with what they have. They don't smile every moment of the day, but then again, who does? There are aspects to life that are unpleasant but have to be dealt with in an adult fashion, understanding it is what it is, completing the task at hand, and then moving on to the next one.

Imagine you see someone coming up the street, making their way with the aid of two canes, dragging their feet along, yet they have that determined look in their eyes of knowing where they are going. Do you feel motivated, perhaps in awe, of such determination?

How about the veteran who comes back from some conflict, having served his country in the fight for freedom and to secure the privilege that you are enjoying at this moment. Do you stop and say, "Thank you"? There he/she is, with missing limbs or damaged in other ways, but again, doing the best one can with what they have.

Or how about that elderly citizen, slowly moving along with a cane or in a wheelchair, worn out from a life of hard work, contributions, paying taxes, and raising a family. Do you offer to open a door for them? Do you help them navigate their way onto a sidewalk, or to load their wheelchair into their vehicle? Really?

Your sense of privilege can become strained as you face your daily challenges. Perspective helps, as well as developing an appreciation for what you have. If you understand that if you want more or something different, and you apply yourself, you can obtain those things you desire.

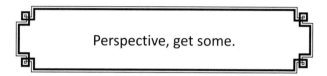

Perspective, get some.

Privilege, do you see it in your life? Can you imagine a life different from what you are currently living? If so, get up and get started, just as all of those before you did, as they exercised their privilege into action.

Think of the song, "Fly Like An Eagle"
by the Steve Miller Band.

: MAKING CHANGES

IT'S ALL AROUND US AND HAPPENS EVERY DAY.

> Resistance to change.
> "Not everything that is faced can be changed;
> But nothing can be changed until it can be faced."

When we say we want change, the term can mean:

- To convert or transform something.

- To become different.

- To undergo transformation, transition, or conversion

- Variety or novelty (as in "for a change")

No matter which way you define it, change is happening all around us and at any given moment.

Some of those changes are orchestrated — as in the ones we invite into our lives — while others may be random — as in the ones that happen without our consent or invitation. How much change do we orchestrate in our lives, or have we hit a wall keeping any kind of change at bay?

For your part, what must be clearly understood is not just how you want to change, but also when this will happen. Once you commit to the changes you need to make, perhaps based on unexpected life events, recent professional downturns or past personal mistakes, why not act on them right now?

Is there a push to go forward with the changes you make, or a pull to resist changes? Within you, what is keeping you resistant? Is it fear, ego, pride, uncertainty, jealousy, or is it a fear of loss? We are driven by a hope of gain or a fear of loss. Which of these two perspectives drive you and your reactions to change?

Where are you on the following diagram?

Quadrant 1: You come in to life in quadrant 1, naked in more ways than one, motivated to do everything. To gain all the required competent skills from childhood onwards, your well-meaning parents or guardians ensure you get some education, mentoring, training and development to stand on your own two legs, literally and figuratively. This phase can last a long time depending on whether you are thrust into the workforce and adulthood before you finish high school, as opposed to moving on to college where you continue to learn. You want to avoid being labeled incompetent, so pressure is on to learn new skills and get on top of things quickly. Life becomes challenging and there can be internal anxiety.

Quadrant 2: This is where you can, and should, remain for as long as you are able to do so. In this quadrant, you have learned to perform a particular job well, or have graduated from college, have landed a job that you want and where you are accepted and rewarded based on your qualifications. You settle down in a place of your liking, associate with friends who best understand you, and lead a disciplined daily life based on appreciation and self-love. In this phase, you are motivated, continue to learn, and build your life around the model you ideally have set in your mind. Life is challenging, but all is well in your world.

Quadrant 3: Life in this particular quadrant indicates a slide in your performance and attitude. Is it because you have not changed and kept up with the times and continued to learn? Or have you simply let yourself slip into mediocrity? At this stage, you are still competent, you know your job or skill sets and can competently perform these whenever you want; the problem is you just don't want to do so, or only when you feel like it. Perhaps your goals have been reached. Or, worse yet, it might be that you have no goals or no motivation to jump out of bed every day and race into action. You can get your mojo back, but you will need to change a few things in your life, or simply re-evaluate your situation and count your blessings. This can happen at any age. You need to be mindful of how easy it is to fall to this level.

Quadrant 4: Once a person gets to this quadrant, it is pretty much a challenge to climb back out. Too often, we see people like this who lose perspective on their own lives, and, instead of taking responsibility, start blaming everyone else as the cause of their misery. These 'woe is me' types talk a good game, but never advance in an attempt to get something done. They have lost the desire to live well, and have fallen out of the employment picture due to many causes, often self-inflicted. It is true that some people suffer as a result of crippling diseases and injuries. But even individuals who fall into this category are able to seek the good in life and continue to apply themselves in a spirit of challenge and conquest. Communication is the key all through one's life, but especially important if you find yourself spiraling into this specific quadrant. If you have hit rock bottom, admit it, communicate your need for help and then support your request with an honest effort.

1. Motivated and incompetent.	2. Motivated and competent.
3. Unmotivated and competent.	4. Unmotivated and incompetent.

Rather than cultivate a "fear of loss" mentality, why not subscribe to a "hope of gain" perspective? Newspapers and online media tend to be filled with articles that often support a "fear of loss" attitude, but why read those stories? You have no influence over the news, other than the news you make.

So ... change is something you have to embrace as an essential part of life.

"For the timid, change is frightening."

"For the satisfied, change is threatening."

"But for the confident, change is opportunity."

- The definition of insanity is doing the same thing and expecting different results. Only change creates different results.

For leaders: You are presently in a position to take charge or in the process of playing such a role. Do you lead the resistance against the invasion of change?

What do you do or what should you do?

- Evaluate what is in progress or coming at you or others.

- Do not say in private what you cannot speak publicly.

- Provide support based on the understanding you have developed through listening and analysis.

- Ensure there is frequent communication to keep people's eyes open.

- Deal promptly and openly with concerns, doubts, and fears.

- Mutually evaluate results with those who suffer from what one might call "change fright."

- Celebrate success. Build up people's confidence once the change has been accepted or dealt with, which in turn leads to greater competence.

Think of the Tears For Fears song, "Change."

Have fun! Change is natural; it keeps us alive and growing.

HAVE YOU TYPE-CASTED YOURSELF? WHY?

What do you think of your abilities to: a) act appropriately within certain situations, b) learn and apply new ways of working, and c) communicate with others?

In your work life, are you capable of doing more than you have done so far? When you apply for work, do you stay within the context of your past accomplishments?

Or do you attempt to work in a new field, try something else, and use your talents and interests in a newer way? Why not? What harm would it do for you to complete an application for a new company, or in a different area of the economy, which require skills that you may not have right now, but are interested in cultivating and developing?

By writing a resumé that looks forward — including a section that expands what you have done, how much you have learned, and what you are willing to do, into what it can mean for the future of your target employer — you will be painting a picture of a person who is ready, willing and able to tackle whatever it takes to make a difference. In the process, you may even bring a fresh perspective to what might be a stodgy and old-thinking company.

Imagine the employer/decision-maker reading your resumé and thinking, "Wow, look at the creativity this person is blessed with and their lack of fear in applying with us, a company that requires skills they do not have in abundance but are willing to apply themselves to learn."

What if you did this? Yes, you. It could mean the dawn of something new for your work life.

Now what about your social/personal life?

Do you find yourself dressing a certain way based on an opinion of yourself, or because you dare not step away from the rest of the herd? Are you happy with that? What is it with fitting in with the rest of the herd that is so appealing? Where is your individuality? Are you a wildebeest, where looking exactly like the rest of the herd reduces the chances a predator will seek you out and eat you?

If you have always taken a narrow view of yourself, it's time to remove the blinders and create a new version of you, based on today's date, current events and current abilities. What is it with being the way you were that is so compelling? Why do you insist in doing the same thing the same way with the same people, which ends up making you predicable to others and, worse, to yourself?

Every day is a new day to try something different.

Like Hollywood movies, Broadway plays and other acting roles, our real lives thrive on those who are flexible in their delivery of words and actions, can take on any number of personalities, and able to quickly mesh in with others.

These actors utilize innumerable assets to help them prepare for each role. With every new challenge they overcome, they gain confidence, new abilities and become well rounded individuals as they perfect their craft.

In a similar vein, our personal lives can mimic such acting roles. Flexibility allows for creativity, which begets more experience and ends up building confidence and competence that you can use in all manner of situations.

How have you cast yourself so far in your life? Can you, or will you, step out of your own shadow and brave the light of day? (I know you can.)

Go ahead. Never mind all those marketing fads enforced by those who cling to a narrow view of life. If you want to be different, then now is the time to be different.

Who and what are you? Right now?

Think of the Richard Branson book, Losing My Virginity.

PERCEPTION & REALITY

On the heels of the last chapter on "typecasting," an important thought comes to mind: Why do you perceive events, news, people, and other things the way that you do?

Why do you staunchly defend your early perceptions, and then shun those people who don't agree with your narrow view of events and the world? Why not instead be open to discussion, lively debate and the chance to learn something new?

Where did you learn that such and such a thing was bad, or wrong, or not for you? Did you really put some thinking into your decision? How long have you been dragging that rock around with you?

Why do you respond quickly when faced with things that seem off or wrong in your view? Do you give people a chance to explain themselves, or are you quick to judge and then move on, leaving those behind you hurt and dazed by your take on "this is the way it is?"

Perception is the ability to see, hear and become aware of something through the senses. You see or hear something and very quickly label it. These labels might include good/bad, useful/useless, expensive/cheap, worth/not worth owning, worth/not worth doing. This same type of behavior can also be applied to the people you meet in which, based on your initial perception, you quickly assign your label of value onto them.

Reality, of course, is not readily evident most of the time. It requires investigation, thinking, discussion and examination to best understand one's reality.

What if you slowed down your transition time from perception to what you think is reality? How would you benefit by being able to dissect new information and then determine whether you want to associate with it?

One-dimensional people act that way, mainly because they often go with their initial decisions based on immediate perceptions. Their inner circle never grows because they stick with only what they know. Time goes by and they miss so many other experiences. Alas, for them, it is what it is — and nothing more.

You, on the other hand, have plenty of choices to make, all day long. Take the time to examine your perceptions before you assign your take on what you think is reality.

It is worth the effort.

Think of the John Conlee song, "Rose Coloured Glasses."

COURSE CORRECTION

When is the right time to make a course correction in your life? If you find that your life is getting too chaotic, or you're being pulled into way too many different directions, when should you do something?

How about now?

Let's say you're a pilot in training. Your aircraft suddenly goes into a downward spiral, heads rapidly toward the ground, and nears the point of an imminent crash. What do you do? As a new pilot, your immediate impulse might be to pull back on the controls. Sounds logical. But … this would prove to be fatal as the aircraft would wind up being torn apart by external G forces and your plane's mechanical/structural limitations.

The correct course of action, in this case, is to apply opposite rudder, and push on the controls. This will take the plane out of its spiral and flatten out the trajectory, which then allows you to pull up before hitting the ground.

This is one of the most difficult lessons for a new pilot to learn. It takes constant repetition before this course of action becomes ingrained as the right thing to do.

What is your correct course of action? Have you been through similar situations in what you are now facing? What did you do? Did it work? Did you crash? Did you survive?

Who can you turn to for guidance on what to do? From that person, will you heed his or her advice? Are you willing to make a proper correction in your life before you spiral to the ground and crash?

The time is always now to make course corrections. But the caveat is that you don't have to have one in order to correct your course. You can steer clear of issues, right?

The biggest obstacle to any course correction is … wait for it … you. Only you can make a correction in your life. The solution is … you guessed it … YOU! Imagine that? You are at your controls. Now learn to fly.

Follow this advice from a George Harrison song by way of Alice In Wonderland author Lewis Carroll: "If you don't know where you are going, any road will take you there."

So … where are you going?

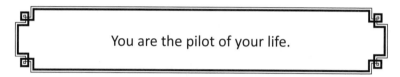

You are the pilot of your life.

Check your headings, head winds, altitude, attitude, and your range to ensure you have a fighting chance to get to where you want to go, and then … take off.

Think of the Alison Krauss song, "Never Got Off The Ground."

MAKING DECISIONS AND COMMITMENTS

Do you make hasty decisions and then just as quickly unmake them? Is deciding what to do a challenge when it comes to finances, the purchase of something expensive like a new car, whether you should date someone you adore, or the millions of other decisions you make throughout your day?

It is acceptable, even normal, to view these types of decisions regarding your future as challenging. You should take your time to weigh all the pros and cons first. Once a decision is made based on enough thoughtful analysis, follow through with that decision.

Too often, you can easily hurt yourself by jumping in and out of situations and/or relationships based on snap choices and the need for instant gratification. As a result, you may lose credibility with others, and soon with yourself, if you make decisions or commitments and then just as easily walk away from them. You end up developing a history that affects those around you and, most of all, yourself.

If you have taken the time and effort to examine all the reasons why something should be, and are comfortable with the decision, then stick to it. This does not mean that you never change your mind if you recognize that what you chose was lacking important details that only came to light later on. It means that there are always competing ideas and options to all the choices you make and you can continually jump from one situation to another while never getting ahead.

Decisions about important details in your life come with solutions that, at first glance, may appear bright and shiny when they are new, exciting because they are different, and thus you find yourself attracted to these new opportunities. The truth is that immediately following your commitment to such decisions is something called hard work and its companion, effort.

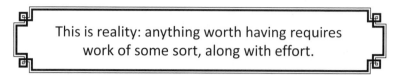

This is reality: anything worth having requires work of some sort, along with effort.

It is not that you are lazy per se, but if you could have known beforehand about what followed that specific decision you made, perhaps you might have chosen a different path. Why, you ask, is the work and the amount of effort to make this decision a part of your life so difficult? Night courses, martial arts, diets, quitting any of the vices you picked up long ago, playing sports with all of the required practices, reading those books that seem so alluring but compete with TV or smartphone time ... so many decisions, but so little time, you say.

Making a decision will require you to replace one thing with something else if your life is to be in balance. What can you move off of your scale in order to add an element that fits and supports your decision? You cannot have it all at the same time; you can have it all if you get or accomplish one thing at a time.

Let's say that you want to become a great guitar player. You made your decision, shopped around and eventually purchased a real nice electric or acoustic model — along with the amplifier, tuner, picks, capo, books — with guidance from the helpful music store clerk. Here you are now staring at the 3,000 chords available for you to use, if you learn how bend your fingers in distorted ways and develop your memory so that you can go from one chord to the other based on the song's specific demands.

You hear one of your favorite songs on the radio and the lead guitar player's riffs leave you awestruck. What do you do now? Well, you made your decision and told everyone about your plan to be a guitar player. Now what? The answer is called work, effort and a commitment. You will practice at least 30 minutes every day on some rudimentary song you like, until you ultimately reach the same level as the players you hear on the radio. When you do these things, you can retire your air guitar career. Instead, you can play the real thing while sitting around the campfire with your friends, or performing on stage at your local bar!

You can do it.

This same thought pattern can apply to any other pursuit or interest you may have, whether you wish to become a model, fly a plane, be a bartender, own a business, or become a doctor. All of these decisions are easy to make right away; it is only what follows the decision that takes maturity, effort, and work.

You must look at the decisions you make in great detail, and understand all of the necessary components that accompany them. Learn to slow down your decision-making process, do the research, understand the work and effort required to make your decision a reality, then go for it!

You can develop a history of making choices and rendering them into reality, becoming a person who "gits 'er dun" and who has confidence and competence as a result.

Think of the Pink Floyd song, "Comfortably Numb."

What decision have you made today?

URGENT VERSUS IMPORTANT

Although we must attend to life's many important tasks and activities, as well as relationships and responsibilities, most of these will fall by the wayside if you are lured by any number of more urgent things that can hold little to no value.

Think about those things you value most in your life: your health, both physical and mental; your family; your job; school; business; friends; as well as hobbies.

Now consider what urgent things conspire to distract you and command your precious time? Emails, texts, social media, TV, movies, alcohol, drugs, loitering about, shopping, spending endless hours looking in the mirror or at the scale ... this list can go on.

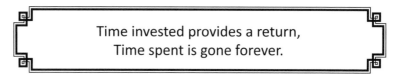

Time invested provides a return,
Time spent is gone forever.

If you attend to those things that are important in your life, you will be successful in a shorter period of time. You can enjoy a full life and feel content knowing you have invested more of your time in activities that pay you back in the form of confidence, competence, love, and, perhaps, financial gain.

If you stick with the urgent stuff, time will be spent, with no return. (A high score on a video game cannot ever compare to having a healthy heart and loving relationships.) One day you will look back and wonder where all your time went and you will ask yourself why you did not recognize that urgent stuff for what it really was.

Well, there is some good news in all this: you do have a choice. You can choose today to become proactive. Say goodbye to your attraction to the urgent stuff. By making the effort and work on what has slowed you, or stopped you, in the past, you have the ability to deal with life's more important matters.

Wait, the news gets even better: you get to choose every day whether or not to "git 'er dun." You can either spend your time with the irresponsible, urgent activities that are easier to do, or get with the program and enjoy the results of time better invested in the important aspects of your life.

Think of the song, "Feeling the Same Way" by Norah Jones.

CIRCLE OF INFLUENCE VERSUS THE CIRCLE OF CONCERN

In the most basic ways to think about your life, you really have two circles that define what you think and do, where you are now and where you will end up.

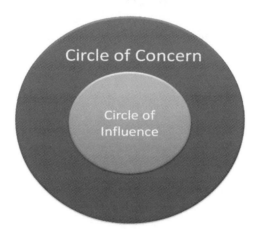

Of the two, the circle of influence should be larger (see diagram above) but all too frequently it resembles a blueberry, while the larger circle of concern winds up looking like a basketball.

Within the circle of influence lies all the things you hold sway over: these can include your health, knowledge, education, skills, abilities, friends, type and quality of work you do, your room or house and the state it is in, your vehicle and how it is maintained, as well as the time you invest in pursuits that bring a reward.

In other words, this circle of influence is you, your choices, your life and how people ultimately will remember you. It is what you have done, along with your words and actions, and the results of your life's efforts.

Thus, your circle of influence is important!

Unfortunately, where people spend and waste most of their time is within the circle of concern, considered to be the urgent useless stuff. But the truth is that you have almost no impact on this circle.

This circle contains less important information like the weather, news, other people's opinions, endless texts, TV shows and what you might call entertainment.

Having a large circle of concern does nothing for you. In fact, it greatly reduces your potency and ends up draining valuable hours that you could have better used elsewhere.

When you take stock of the time you spend in this circle, you begin to see that all of it is in vain — that it offers no value, and has no merit. The news of today is the same as the news from last week, last year or a decade ago. Just take a newspaper from the past, change the date to today, and alarmingly you will note that the stories are nearly all the same.

Gold prices are up, gold prices are down; crime is up, crime is down; wars are everywhere; the costs of living, housing, groceries, and more are rising; the stock market is unstable … really, take a look at this endless waste of words.

Your challenge, then, is to invest as much of your time in your circle of influence in order that you achieve what you set out to do with your life.

> If you want to change your life and maximize on your time and talents, turn away from the distractions.

Focus on what you can impact, enhance your ability to do more using technology for your benefit only.

The circle of concern (urgent) will always be there, buzzing like flies outside the screen of your room. You can open the screen and let in those pesky insects, you can ignore them, or you can even close the window thereby eliminating the sound they make and limiting the effect they have on you.

Stay with the circle of influence (important), because you are important and are developing what is your life.

Is it selfish of you to do the best you can with what you have? I don't think so, nor should you.

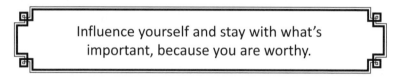

Influence yourself and stay with what's important, because you are worthy.

Think of you — yes, you! Think of what you think about, can you see which circle you spend most of your time in? Draw two circles, and fill them in with the words that apply per this section. This exercise will help awaken you.

Think of the Al Stewart song, "A Man For All Seasons."

"STUPID IS AS STUPID DOES"? NOT QUITE.

Recognize that line from the movie, "Forrest Gump?" It's a line that gets stated quite a few times from the film's main character, wonderfully played by Tom Hanks.

I mutate that particular line into this: "Smart is as smart does."

There are plenty of smart people out there, but some of them simply do not use their intelligence wisely. There are other people who may not be extremely gifted mentally, yet some are able to get more done with their lives, deploy more discipline and maximize on their time.

> Doing smart things requires you to know and accept what needs to be done, and then doing it.

Take tithing, for example. Make yourself the recipient by paying yourself that first 10 percent of your income, which can be invested in something you enjoy in your later years. Retiring with some money is a good thing, and others will go on to say how smart you were as a result of applying this financial discipline. But honestly, being smart had nothing to do with it. Or did it?

Examine the life of someone who studies and learns various trades and skills and then watch the returns they enjoy from their early efforts. They end up earning a substantial paycheck, live a life as defined by them, are never out of work, and people will talk about how smart they were.

Look at musicians or actors who following years of practice and study go on to enjoy a great living in the spotlight. They worked hard, overcame any fears of public speaking and acting and benefited from their efforts. Some smarts likely were required, but it was work and focus that earned them all the accolades.

None of those people are necessarily the smartest. What they have done is selected activities and pursuits that interested them, worked hard, and enjoyed the returns on their invested time.

There are also extremely successful people who just happen to be caught up in such vices as drug and alcohol abuse, smoking, or eating disorders, that cause them so many unnecessary hardships. These people may also turn out to be smart, but the point is that being smart in and of itself doesn't guarantee you will be happy and successful.

Using your smarts in a constructive way, in a consistently effort-filled fashion, and throughout your lifetime will bring you the rewards you seek. What counts the most is the focus and deliberate action you apply toward an attainable goal or passion.

By reading, thinking, planning, working and doing the best you can with what you have, you will be successful, by your standards. That is the smart thing to do.

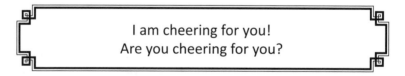

Think of the movie, "Forrest Gump," with Tom Hanks.
(Entertaining and smarter than you think.)

SPENDING VERSUS INVESTING TIME

Do you spend your time or invest it? Once you spend your money. it is gone. The same can be said of time.

Think of the term, "killing time," and how often you have been guilty of saying or thinking, "Well … I only have one more hour to kill before I get to do …" whatever it is you are waiting to do. But what could you do with that hour? You could certainly finish a job at work, clean your work space, write an important follow-up memo, practice music, iron your clothes, speak to a family member, read, work in the garden, take a brisk walk … whatever works best for you.

Are you familiar with the story of the person concerned about his or her failing health who visits the doctor, and the doctor comes back into the room and says, "You need to exercise," to which the patient replies, "but, Doctor, I don't have time to exercise!" The doctor calmly retorts, rather sardonically, "Oh, I see. Do you have time to die?"

Would it not be better to invest some of your time into those things that will make your life healthier, more productive and more appreciated?

Let's use golf, tennis, weightlifting, music as examples of activities most of us don't get paid to do. Yet people will spend countless hours on the golf course or putting green, in the weight room, with music teachers or with friends, constantly practicing and improving in these activities.

What about learning more about your job? Seek out a mentor if you are not assigned one, and learn as much as you can about the one thing that puts money in your pockets, food on your plate, toys under the Christmas tree for your kids …

There is nothing wrong with the other activities. But for some reason, people go to work just to work and mostly do not invest their time to learn as much as they can.

Treating work like an investment seems to be a prudent thing to do, as opposed to a place where you spend your time.

Do you have any spare time? Really?

Think of the Bodil Jonsson book, Unwinding The Clock.

YOUR PERSONAL SCALE

You are unique and different from everyone else in the world, aren't you?

What suits one person does not always apply to another? What your co-workers, family or friends want or do, may or may not be what you want to do. Or, more importantly, what you should do with your life. What things are important to you, for which you would not make any compromises?

What are your minimum requirements when it comes to work, nutrition, private time, earning potential, effort, and love? What are those things you expect from your significant other? Do they know? Are you clear on what these minimums are? If they are clear to you, are they just as clear to those within your circle?

Your scale is yours. What dreams, desires and goals you put on your personal side of the scale are things that apply to you, and are later used to measure or balance against the opportunities, prospects and what you are willing to achieve. In its simplest form, you can hold out your hands in front of you when speaking with someone regarding an option under consideration. And, as you are listening to them, load up your side of the scale (that is, your hand) and then load up the other side/hand and see whether they balance.

If one side is not budging or clearly being outweighed, then you need to look deeper to ensure you have balanced your side of the scale based on your reality, or take everything off the scale having decided that this particular option is simply not for you.

> **Things in life need to balance out, which means considering all aspects of your options.**

It helps to visualize these scales as you think because too often we make hasty decisions out of balance with our side of the scale. Too often, a good friend, family member, or even one's boss might have us do tasks that are simply not in our best interest. When this happens, whose fault is it?

Think of this as justice for you in the long and short term. Just as in negotiating contracts or fair deals, you will be better armed if you have taken the time (in the gap) to consider the options, benefits, costs, amount of pain versus pleasure, etc., before you agree or disagree.

The utilitarian concept, in a shortened definition, explains that you need to consider how many units of pain versus how many units of pleasure each situation offers. It may sound simple, but at least it has you thinking about balancing the scales, for right now as well as later in your life.

Is your life in balance? Are you too easily swayed? Can it be said that you are a pushover and easily exploited?

Think of the Fleetwood Mac song, "Go Your Own Way."

STICK TO THAT COMMITMENT

What are you committed to doing? What commitments are you working on now?

Commitment is the bedrock of any meaningful relationship between you, a significant other, your team, your employer and those for whom you agree to perform a particular action or function.

Decisions are constantly made and can be changed depending on what happens next. Commitments require work in order to understand what is required ahead of time. (Only someone who is being foolish will commit to something they do not understand.)

The most important commitment you can make is to yourself. Once made, you must have the strength of character to stick to that commitment, come hell or high water. The problem with commitments is that they usually involve work, effort, restraint, discipline, and other strenuous activities. Most people prefer to take the easy road of mediocrity, whereby people let others off easily once promises are not kept, and commitments, especially to oneself, are not followed through, even if a person suddenly remembers them afterward.

At one time, business was done on a handshake. Deals were made and delivery of promised goods or services occurred without fail or delay. People's words meant something, and were used judiciously in the small communities where they lived. Today, with business and life occurring at the speed of a thought, commitments need to be secured in writing, sometimes with the use of a lawyer, and, if necessary, monitored and enforced.

What about you? Do you require a written covenant to remind you to keep your word, and then self-enforce your words should you not deliver?

Have you made any commitments to yourself? What are they? Have you kept them? What has resulted from your commitment? Each time you make a commitment and then support it with action, does your self-confidence grow stronger? It should.

Promises are easy to make. Just look at New Year's Eve promises, wishes, hopes, dreams ... and you can see how simple these can be said out loud, but also unfortunately how long such so-called commitments last.

Making true commitments falls entirely on a different level. An example would be one's marriage vows — formal commitments from both parties to live by the spirit of the union in which they are engaging, and doing all the necessary things that make a couple's union endure the test of time. In the case of marriage, too many people say these vows without really understanding what they mean and how they must live up to them in the face of ever-changing circumstances.

A true commitment to oneself or others needs to be based on knowledge of what the commitment means, what it will take to live up to it, and what negative consequences might result should you fail to uphold it.

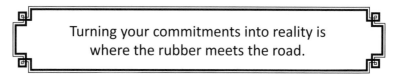

Turning your commitments into reality is where the rubber meets the road.

So ... what commitments are you going to make with yourself, and that you will turn into reality through your effort, work and determination? Earn a defined income? Buy a home by a certain date? Achieve straight-As in the school you attend? Become proficient on a musical instrument? Build a profitable company?

The No. 1 obstacle to keeping commitments is you.

The No. 1 solution to keeping commitments is you.

You Working With You

Think of the Burton Cummings song, "Stand Tall."

Make a commitment to love yourself, and build the life you want for you based on that love. After all, you always treat those things you love, with love, don't you?

DISCIPLINE, OR MORE IMPORTANTLY, SELF-DISCIPLINE (DON'T EVER GET TIRED OF THIS WORD — EVER!)

If there is one word throughout this book, or any other self-help book, coaching manuals, diet solutions, music lessons, how-to books … it is discipline, with the major proviso being SELF-DISCIPLINE.

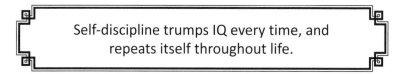

Self-discipline trumps IQ every time, and repeats itself throughout life.

While being impulsive might seem fun, what will add better value to your life is the ability to set a course, attend to the details, and then do whatever it takes to get there.

Take a look at the world's great guitarists, actors, pilots, machinists, race car drivers, salespeople or just about anyone else who is successful at what they do or are comfortable in their own skin. How did they all get to be this great? It just took one common element: discipline.

An undisciplined life leaves you running about like a chicken with its head cut off. Undisciplined people are susceptible to every whim or fancy that comes their way. They are always looking for validation in their quest to establish self-worth, and, among other things, their speech patterns are often not well-thought out, but rather formed by just blurting out whatever passes through their minds.

- Discipline will have you do the right things at the right time in your life, for all the right reasons.

- Discipline will have you choose between possible outcomes, having considered what is required to achieve the desired result, as opposed to just throwing yourself at every opportunity that comes along.

- Discipline will have you think and, at times, do nothing because perhaps that is the best course of action at that moment. Doing nothing can be considered as much a choice as selecting to do something — the difference is that only you know why.

- Discipline will have you eating more nutritiously and being mindful of what you put into your body, regardless of who is encouraging you to do otherwise.

- Discipline will have you fit and feeling good as a result of choosing activity over inactivity driven by the likes of TV, computers and games, texting, loitering about …

- Discipline will contribute to you taking the time to think things through, by carving out time out of your busy day, time to be silent and allow balance to occur.

- Discipline and the power of will are both very worthwhile tools to have in your tool chest.

If there is one wish I have for you is that you develop, and keep on developing, your discipline and apply it towards the goals and interests that make you what you are — a unique person. Don't be afraid to be on the edge. You don't need the approval of others, do you?

Be you.

Think of you, your life, your choices and where you hope those will lead you. As Forrest Gump once said, "Life is like a box of chocolates."

PRACTICE
(10,000 HOURS: MALCOLM GLADWELL)

In his book *Outliers*, author Malcolm Gladwell chronicles some of the successful people who have benefited from their investment of time into practice, knowledge and the skill required to achieve the level of success that they did. These successful people earned the rewards they obtained through good old-fashioned work, effort and practice.

> Anything worth doing, is worth doing well.
> Yes or no?

When you were in grade school, you practiced and memorized everything: Mathematics until you mastered it, geography until you could navigate the globe, history until you could see the patterns of mistakes repeated over and over. (Not that history ever repeats itself in your life …)

Since school what have you learned? What have you practiced? What are you really good at doing?

If you want harmony in your life, and between those with whom you interact, you will see a noticeable difference in the quality of your relationships if you apply effort and practice. Practice listening, being polite, playing the sports in which you want to participate, cooking those dishes that others can enjoy, and doing the many things that make you the unique person that you are.

Practice may sound like an odd word when applied to everyday tasks. But what other word captures the essence of what it takes to get better at doing something, anything?

Repetition is key, whether playing an instrument or sport, public speaking, fixing mechanical equipment, working with software, washing dishes or cleaning a house. The more you do it, the better you become — that is, if better is where you are bound.

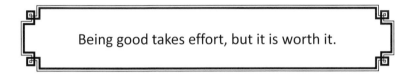
Being good takes effort, but it is worth it.

If your goal is to be in a certain job position, then you should start now if you have not already done so, to learn and be all of the things that such a job position requires.

Certainly there is some on-the-job learning, technology that will change, and so on.

But that pilot of a 747 jet airliner with 500 people on board is quite confident and will not require a book in mid-flight to help him with his next decision or course change.

And yet there are those among us who whine about the world not being fair. Just watch those people: Do they walk the walk? Have they applied themselves over time in order to reach their intended goal? The two key words in this paragraph are "over time," as many people have a great idea, work at achieving it for a week or two, (maybe three) then … move onto the next thing.

The life you want is there for you. It never will be handed over on a silver spoon, but it is there. Practice your skills and abilities and then go out and compete for those things you want. You may not win at everything, but you will win at obtaining some of the things you want.

Think of the Bob Rotella book, How Champions Think.

NUTRITION AND CONSUMPTION

There have been thousands of books and magazines dedicated to dieting. Television and radio talk-show hosts earn millions of dollars discussing the latest fads. Counsellors make a living "helping" people lose weight. Acupuncture, pills, special diets, weight-loss companies are all readily available … and for what?

The problem is that most people are unaware of what it feels like to be hungry. And I mean truly hungry. Even if the digestive system/stomach (think of a tube) is full, the moment the level of food drops, gluttonous people continually rush to top it up … as if they are programmed to keep their bellies constantly full.

Your body can live over 21 days without any food. Mahatma Gandhi survived more than three weeks in total starvation (he did drink water) and lived.

How long have you gone without eating? Really? Keep a diary of when and what you eat, for 30 days.

(Water is different; 60 percent of your body is water and every cell needs it to function and survive.)

Why do you think there are so many fast-food outlets, food trucks, machines dispensing food, takeout and delivery, and restaurants? People cannot drive by one without stopping in to top off their tube, when in reality their tube has enough food in it to last between one to three weeks!

Are people really afraid of starving to death if they do not give into these impulses driven by marketing and bad habits? Will the fat police come and take them away if they do not fill up their quota?

Your body and mind need to live. When you say yes to good health, you also say yes to sizes of clothing you want to wear, a certain weight based on body mass and height, to good fresh vegetables, fruits and healthy choices of food, to an active lifestyle, and to feel proud that you can actually say no to a life of inactivity and unhealthy junk food.

You have the ability to do everything you want in your life, consecutively, but you cannot do it all at the same time, or concurrently. You cannot take a walk and watch TV; you cannot play a sport and be on social media; you cannot drive your car and text; you cannot fit into clothing that you want to wear and eat fast food every day; you cannot take a night course or study for a subject that will help you earn more money and party with your friends every night.

Just say yes to one, and automatically the other gets a firm, "No!"

When you think of dieting and nutrition, you ignore an essential part of your body, and that would be your ... mind. What are you thinking? Right now? Do you see yourself as you want to be? Are you thinking good thoughts? Are you using your mind for good purposes and are fully engaged in your life?

Nutrition, good health, fun, true laughter, friends, activities, strong body and mind — these all can lead to success. None of these will come to you through your electronic devices, computers, tablets, social media, movies, or television. All it takes is some solid thinking and doing those things you truly want to do.

Our world is based on consumption, the message from all the companies that profit greatly from everything you shove into your body, put on your body, or use is that you need more, and more, and more!

Do you? Really? Why? Who is in charge of you anyway? Them?

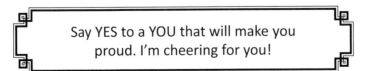

Say YES to a YOU that will make you proud. I'm cheering for you!

Richard Morin

Think of the Neil Diamond song, "Song Sung Blue."

Or,

for a laugh, the song, "Feed Me" from the movie, "Little Shop of Horrors."

DISTRACTIONS

Are you able to focus and "git 'er dun"?

When you are given a task, can you round up the tools, information, or colleagues you need to complete the required job on time?

Is this something you can work with and improve? What impedes you as you set out to start and finish a task?

Some extol the virtues of multitasking. But show me someone who has several tasks on the go, piled up on their desk or stacked up on their monitor, and I will show you someone who needs to knock one off at a time and then move on to the next one.

When a request arrives in front of you, deal with it, delegate it, or put it into your calendar with a firm deadline date if that is the best course of action. Do not let these requests stack up with the rest of the work and other tasks that take up your day.

It is true that some tasks require waiting for approval, for further information to be completed, for the necessary permits, or whatever. But for the most part, distractions that impede our productivity are, in fact, manageable.

If someone approaches you and requests to have a minute of your time, ask that person if a minute is enough. If you get a deer-in-the-headlights look and a stammering response, then ask if it can wait and schedule a time later in the day — when you have the time that inquisitive person needs — to deal with his or her specific question or issue.

If you are going to hold a meeting, make a clear agenda with suggested time allocations, send it out to those who "need" to be there, in advance so that they can prepare and contribute. Then run your meeting the way you planned it. If other points come up, stay the course and deal with those new ideas at a follow-up meeting.

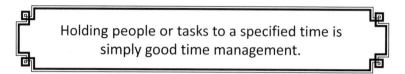

Holding people or tasks to a specified time is simply good time management.

If you have the audible whip as an incoming message indicator on your electronic device, then disable it. Will it matter if you check your messages every hour or two instead of being at everyone's beck and call?

Distractions, you say? Who is driving your life? You? Then take control before you crash.

Think of the Napoleon Hill book, The Law of Success.

BLINDERS

We put blinders on horses in order to keep them from being skittish or nervous, as these narrow their visual focus to merely what is straight ahead of them. Their use makes it safer for the rider or those in the wagon. (Sucks to be the horse, though.)

What about you? Do you want what is safe? Are you comfortable staying in the middle of the road, with no peripheral view? Are you sure you are not wearing blinders? Has someone or some group of people who, conspiring through their opinions, comments, looks, and direct admonitions, made you believe that you should only look straight ahead, and not be distracted by all of the other activities and opportunities around you?

Here you are, a creative, thinking person. But for some reason, you remain on the same path in your life, never straying from the well-worn trail you take every day.

If this is the path that you have chosen and are blissfully pleased with this route, then good for you! There's a lot to be said for the person who is doing exactly what they want, and doing it well at the exclusion of all else.

If this path leaves you dissatisfied, bored and unfulfilled, and you would like to stray from the road you are currently travelling, then open your eyes wide, remove the visual constraints and take a look at all the other options that exist for you.

At first glance, these options seem too arcane or different from your current life, and they include work in order to be able to harness them, understand them, and make them a part of you, your skills, or life in general. If work is not something in which you want to engage, then perhaps keeping the blinders on might be a good idea.

If, however, you have the ability to work and are willing to see what you can accomplish with your life, then looking around and taking on new challenges will be a good thing and can teach you a lot about yourself.

What do you have to lose? You can always return to the more familiar path — it will always be there for you. If you want something more or something different, don't just jump without considering the outcome — at least take the time to examine the different ways that will lead to your ending.

Examine why you think the way you do, and the limitations you feel are yours, and you will find that you might have been wearing virtual blinders that have kept you oblivious to anything else other than just what was happening directly in front of you.

*Think of the Clint Black song, "We Tell Ourselves"
or the Elton John song, "Circle of Life."*

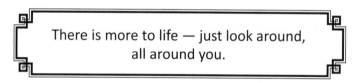

There is more to life — just look around, all around you.

Can you think of someone who needs to consider what you have just read? What will you do now?

HABITS, ACCORDING TO CHARLES DUHIGG

When you look at what you do daily, weekly or monthly, you will see that to a large extent you are a creature of habit.

It goes without saying that good habits are good and, by extension, bad habits are, well, bad.

Eating habits, exercise habits, thinking habits where you are always the victim, work habits, social habits, consumption habits … in short, we are habitual beings.

Exercise? Acting legend Bob Hope is known to have said: "Whenever I get the urge to exercise, I lay down until it goes away." (The man did live until he was 100 years old. He was, after, all, a boxer, played golf, and exercised.)

What are your habits? What do you do in your day and are you surprised when you reach the end of each day and try to remember at what points you actually chose a thought or action?

If you want a good habit, and your day is full, you need to lose a bad habit, which you can define as one that takes up so much of your time but results in nothing.

Try this list of how you can replace your bad habits with better ones:

- Instead of watching or listening to the news first thing in the morning, go for a walk or run, get on the floor and do some yoga or exercise.

- Instead of checking out all of the media you habitually read, review the day in front of you, plan, prepare, and get ready to live in the moment.

- Once you arrive at work, get right to work. Do those harder tasks first, preferably early in the day, or early in your shift.

- Instead of plopping down on the couch when you get home, having a drink, or turning on the TV, get active. Clean up the garage, pick up that mess that threatens to engulf you, find a recipe and get cooking, go for a walk where you can ramp up your vigour and have time for you in order to regain your balance.

- Instead of smoking 25 times a day (is there anything else in your life that you do as often as smoke cigarettes? Other than breathe? Really?) Do something, anything.

Other than cultivating the habit of silence, you might also consider reading. Yes, you read it here first.

I've heard it said: "The people who do not read are no better off than those who cannot read." This may sound a little harsh, even judgmental, but given the choice and the ability, is it not true that one is better off reading, and it is a habit that is worth having?

Habits? Do you have any?

Think of the Charles Duhigg book, The Power of Habits.

INFORMATION GATHERING OR SOLUTION MODE?

People buy books for many reasons, and the author of course writes books in most cases because he has a story in him, or an axe to grind, or perhaps he wants to take a biographical approach as he feels as though he has a lesson to share, or an experience to pass on to others.

I narrow down the spectrum of reasons to read to either entertainment/information-gathering or because someone is in solution mode.

In entertainment/information-gathering mode, the individual is simply engaged in reading for recreation, and enjoying their escape into the book. Their situation is what it is and they are OK with that. They read, perhaps learn something, laugh, and apply what they have read to their lives — or not. It is all up to them.

Fiction books, for example, are mostly about entertainment, although some of these writings have huge amounts of research going into them and thus have high value contained in them.

In solution mode, the reader is seeking an answer, looking for the light, straining to learn and understand life and how they fit in, where they might go and how they might improve their lot in life. Perhaps with pen and paper in hand or by writing and highlighting passages in the book, they learn and capture the essence of what the book means to them. They find pearls of wisdom contained in the book as it relates to them and as a result are better off having consumed and digested the book in question.

A lot of readers have not thought about whether they are in either camp and perhaps at the outset a book can be very entertaining and fun to read, but later on it takes on the form of a reference book, one where the reader associates with the message or content and takes on a thought process created as a result of reading.

Life is like that, there are messages and signs all along the trail of life, it is up to us to be open to them and even seek them out.

When the student is ready, the teacher will appear.

Think of the A.C. Grayling book, The Reason of Things *specifically the chapter on Identity.*

COURAGE

Courage is going from one failure to another, without losing enthusiasm. (Hopefully, learning as you go along.)

Do you require courage in order to live in this day and age? Yes!

Now, in dramatic fashion you might think that a soldier in the line of fire needs a higher level of courage to stand up and shoot at the enemy never knowing if an incoming bullet will find him, and that this kind of courage is very different than the courage you need to live your life. But think about it: A soldier is trained to do what he does, is a professional, volunteered to be there, and as the numbers bear out, most of them survive and go on to fight another day. And yes it does take courage, a lot of it.

You are also trained to do what you do. If you keep up the training and learning, you will develop courage — which comes in part from confidence and competence that will aid you in your performance, and allow you to live the way you want.

You need the courage to stand up on your own and do those things that others might not condone, or be willing to take part of. You need courage to apply for challenging jobs that will stretch you in new ways, and once you learn and master the new opportunity, you need more courage to take a leap at the next level, and the next until you reach your "real" comfort zone.

Courage, what have you done lately that was dangerous in a way, a strain on your nerves and something that your so called friends and peers warned you, not to do?

Think of the Allison Krauss song, "Crazy as Me."

What goal or challenge will you step into now?

BELIEVING, AFTER ALL, REQUIRES SO MUCH LESS EFFORT THAN THINKING.

Have you ever duped a child? Told them a story that is simply not true? Played a trick on them that left everybody laughing, including the child? There they are, staring at you with eyes wide open, listening to your every word, watching your body language and believing that what you are telling them is the truth.

Have faith and trust in people, because their message and what they stand for is one of the foundations of a healthy life. By the same token, you simply should not, or cannot, believe everything that everybody says. (Dichotomy?)

Being gullible is not a good characteristic to hone. You should develop your ability to ask questions that will bridge the gap between mere acceptance and the correct answers that meet your needs.

It is a fine balance that you must be aware of and realize that there are two sides to the scales you use in your life. On one end of the scale are the words, actions, products, promises and such that come at you every day. On the other end is you, your needs, your financial wherewithal, your beliefs, well-being and your ability to discern whether the other side of the scale has value, applies to you, and is truly in your best interests.

In order to acquire that balance, you must apply thinking to what makes the most sense for you. Go ahead and ask lots of questions. Based on your trust level of the person doing the speaking, do his or her words, actions or beliefs always apply to you? Will you be better off believing everything that others are saying, or doing what they ask of you? It might make sense from someone else's perspective, but perhaps that same talk doesn't necessarily fit your ever-developing profile. This is about you, right?

If you are reading this, you are probably not a child. By now you might be smiling at the way you no longer are falling for people who lied to you. Knowing what you know now, you may be questioning the products that did not deliver, or the job descriptions that might hide the truth of what tasks are truly required from you.

This topic is filled with controversy based on how blind trust has played into your life. From the time you were a child, you were taught to believe your parents, teachers, religion, government, rules, regulations and an endless list of static laws governing all aspects of your life.

But, how wise is it to simply believe without questioning everything we hear, read and see? How often do we find out in hindsight that the person we once respected and trusted turned out to be not only wrong, but also willfully lied to us over great periods of time, their motivations purely for their own gain?

When you are speaking with someone and telling them about an event or thought you have, you might not enjoy a thousand or more questions coming your way concerning the validity of what you just said. But why not enjoy the questions that people throw back at you? It would provide you a chance to elaborate, and if some aspect of what you said was inaccurate, you could admit it and learn as a result.

The greatest inventions in history come from people not believing that a particular product or situation was sacrosanct. They questioned, then they believed the new reality they created in part through their questioning.

Empires have fallen, religions with their abuse of power and the trust people had placed in them have crumbled, entire governments have been toppled by the power of questions and the search for truth from those not afraid to stand up and question what is being said or the value proposition being offered.

Believing is good, knowing is better. Believe in yourself, in your ability to get along with life, your strength and purpose, the future you are working towards, and know that every day is a new day, literally, in all aspects of your life. Develop a love of self, and protect that love.

This book is about you, and the belief you have in yourself and the love you carry with you. Questions are one thing, doubts are another.

Think of the Elton John song, "Believe."

Believe in you!

Can you think of someone you need to confront and engage in an honest exchange based on questions you have of them? Is it time to stand up? Now?

WHAT'S HOLDING YOU BACK? YOU?

Before you can answer this, you have to have an idea of what you want to do. If nothing is what you want to do, then there is nothing or very little holding you back.

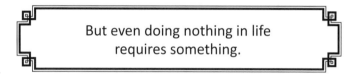

But even doing nothing in life requires something.

You have to have a place in which to do nothing. Within this place, there needs to be heat, food and water along with bathing facilities. To do nothing will require you to have clothes and of course a facility to clean them. And, oh yes, there is that little thing called money, usually earned through work (although there are other avenues), which you will need to spend in order to pay for this place where you will do nothing.

So you see, doing nothing is not an option; you will have to work or in some way pay for those things just mentioned.

Have you, or do you, want to define your life, your time on this beautiful planet we call Mother Earth?

What do you want to accomplish? What skills do you want to learn? Which musical instruments do you want to play? Where do you want to travel? In which locations would you want to live? How many children do you want to have?

Have you identified the biggest obstacle and also the solution to the obstacle? (The answer could be ... you? Yes or no?)

Do you recognize that the largest and yet most flexible obstacle is ... you? Do you realize that your efforts are the solution to overcoming all of your obstacles, issues and challenges?

What is holding you back? Why are you doubtful of what you can do or accomplish? Who told you that you were limited or that you lacked abilities sufficient to get done in this life what you want to get done?

Do you believe that you are equal to everyone else? Are you aware of how all the people who are termed "successful" overcame their obstacles? When asked, they will readily admit that the opportunities were always there and that to get the desired results, they had to apply themselves to prove that they could, as the saying goes, "git 'er dun."

Stop looking for excuses, eliminate the negative self-talk that has brought you to this point and choose instead to think good thoughts, constructive thoughts, thoughts of success and accomplishment.

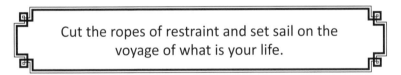

> Cut the ropes of restraint and set sail on the voyage of what is your life.

Think of the movie, "Million Dollar Baby" directed by Clint Eastwood.

WHY NOT YOU, WHY NOT NOW? (BE, HAVE, LEARN, ENJOY, SEE, HEAR, TASTE, WORK ... NOW)

Why not you? Why not me? Why not now? What stands in the way? You may not live a fairy tale life, but you can certainly live a life that has more of what you want and less of what you don't want. Can't you? Why not you? Why not now?

> Think, plan and work towards those things that will make your life what you, want it to be, when you want it to be.

What you have done up to now has brought you to this point. Just imagine what more focus, effort and work will do for you.

Think of all of the people who have lived full lives — the way they wanted to live. Now immediately you will want to think of the famous people who grace the TV and movie screens, or on the glossy front pages of magazines.

But let's not forget that there are plenty of successful commoners who lived very fulfilled lives raising a family on a farm that they dreamed of owning. There are many truckers who lived the dream as they saw it. Owning a home, raising children, and being their own boss by being a driver or an owner-operator.

What about the accountant who goes to university or college for years in order to serve clientele willing to pay for his or her services? He or she lives as he wants, takes vacations, and does the work that he or she always wanted to do and studied hard to become competent in this field.

There are as many examples as there are people. There are also those who simply refused to define their objectives and their lives, and then grumble how everything was stacked against them. But was it, and is it now? What can they do to help themselves now?

So, why not you? Have you planned? Have you thought of what it is you will do with your hours, days, months, years and decades of your life?

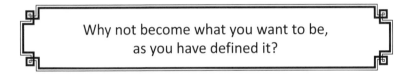

Why not become what you want to be, as you have defined it?

The reality is that you can become what you want, and then decide that there is something else you want to do more, then do that, and then move into something completely different again. You can do this countless times — providing you continue to apply yourself, learn, work and do the best you can with what you have.

You don't need to hang onto a job that you hate just because you want to draw a pension for your eventual retirement some 20 or 30 years from now.

Be what you want by defining what is required and then doing the work it takes to get there.

Why not you? Why not now?

Think of the Pink Floyd song, "Wearing The Inside Out."

THE END

TA DAAA, finished, whew, sigh, yawn and stretch, pick up the next book, or … get up and get something done? Better yet, go back through the book, to those sections or captured thoughts that you highlighted and now need to dig up and add to the ingredients that make up your life?

What now?

Will you lend your copy to a friend or someone you think can use the information or motivation, or will you order a few copies for your family, co-workers, employees, etc.?

Is the end of this book a beginning based on some new thoughts and ideas concerning time, your life and the things you want to get done before you reach the end of your own life/book? Or does it go on the heap and now you are on to the next one?

What are the things you want to accomplish with your life?

Go ahead and list those things here:

- Goals?

- Projects?

- New ideas as to what you will do with today and the days that follow this one?

- A clear amount of money you want to retire with?

- The kind of house or residence you want to reside in?

- Perhaps a company you want to start or own that does business in a particular type of industry, it might be B2B or B2C.

- A target of fitness ability including doing an iron man, or marathon, or simply bicycling on vacation in a far-away destination.

- Building a family with a particular mate in mind.

- Playing a musical instrument.

- Learning to cook a new dish.

- Or …

I don't know about you, but for me this life has been a hell of a ride, and it just keeps on keeping on, with new experiences falling into place, or being dragged into play through my effort and energy applied.

My hope is that you will finish your life having awarded yourself a graduation certificate cum laude.

Because you are reading this, you still are still alive, hence hence still have time. Time to _____ you fill in the blanks.

What a life!

EPILOGUE

DEATH: A TABOO SUBJECT FOR SOME?

Death like birth is what it is. It happens.

You don't want to be cold about it, but for something that we all know is inevitable, you can be more pragmatic about it and perhaps accelerate your pace while the sun is still shining, on you.

I have grieved for lost loved ones, good friends and even for people whom I never met, but whose ending was tragic. I have cried buckets of tears and questioned life about why bad things have to happen, and the reasons why we must pass on. But it happens in spite of all the tears and questions.

You will have to learn to accept things with time and experience, yes, you will have concern for others, but … sadly no real influence, and without an answer to the call of death.

I read that death is like a little guy riding on your shoulder. Nobody else can see him, but you know he is there. You can feel his warm embrace as he hugs your head and whispers into your ear, "Don't worry, we will be together soon enough. Go about your day, every day and enjoy this life. When it is time, I will be here with you. Don't worry, we will be together."

The moral of this story? Simply live, without worry, as your future is assured.

With the certainty of death on your horizon, and the amount of time that basic living requirements take out of your day, it is a shame to run out of time on your quest to achieve those things you want to complete before you are united with that aforementioned little guy.

What is important to you, in your life? Have you been buried in the minutia of the urgent? Are you working within your circle of influence (you) or trapped in the growing circle of concern?

Should there be urgency in your gait?

I am still here, writing and exploring life as I go, working towards the achievement of my goals, where I will wind up nobody knows. I wish you well on your journey and hope that you think good thoughts, live a good life defined by you, and that you have no regrets when you lay down for the final time.

He is patiently awaiting you, biding his time. While you are applying your time to those things you want to accomplish. Choose well.

Namaste,

ABOUT THE AUTHOR

Richard Morin is a bon vivant who enjoys writing, speaking, training, motivating and inspiring others through his words and actions. He runs two companies while representing others in the North American Market.

Having lived eight years in the United States where Richard managed the sales for two fortune 500 companies, and travelling throughout much of the world, he has influenced many people who went on to become clients / customers, associates, allies, partners and friends.

Richard's ambition is to influence people to be all they can be, and to challenge the status quo as it applies to each individual, which is as different as the person is from others.

This is his second book, the first never saw the light of day as he succumbed to the doubt and lack of confidence he faced during that period. Writing this book came at a different time in his life, hence is now a completed work, one should never give up.

Richard is married to his beautiful wife Sylviane, having four children between them. He invests his time in writing books and songs, reading, riding his bicycle, exercising, cooking and playing guitar.